Threshold 1990

Threshold 1990

Council of Europe
Conseil de l'Europe

J. A. van Ek and J. L. M. Trim

PUBLISHED BY THE PRESS SYNDICATE OF THE UNIVERSITY OF CAMBRIDGE
The Pitt Building, Trumpington Street, Cambridge CB2 1RP, United Kingdom

CAMBRIDGE UNIVERSITY PRESS
The Edinburgh Building, Cambridge CB2 2RU, United Kingdom
40 West 20th Street, New York, NY 10011–4211, USA
10 Stamford Road, Oakleigh, Melbourne 3166, Austrailia

Printed in the United Kingdom at the University Press, Cambridge

A catalogue record for this book is available from the British Library

Library of Congress Cataloguing in Publication data applied for

ISBN 0 521 56706 8 paperback

Table of contents

Preface

Threshold is the latest, thoroughly revised, extended, corrected and reset version of *The Threshold Level* by Dr. J. A. van Ek, first published by the Council of Europe in 1975 as part of a project to investigate the feasibility of a unit/credit system for adult language learning in Europe. The Project Group set out to develop conceptual and planning instruments to assist teachers and course planners to analyse the needs of the learners towards whom they had responsibilities and to set, consciously and explicitly, appropriate learning objectives.

Learning objectives will, in principle, be as diverse as the learners and the lives they lead. However, large-scale educational systems have to base their provision on learners' common needs. By far the largest single group of language learners everywhere consists of people who want to prepare themselves to communicate socially with people from other countries, exchanging information and opinions on everyday matters in a relatively straightforward way, and to conduct the necessary business of everyday living when abroad with a reasonable degree of independence. *The Threshold Level* was the first attempt to set out in systematic detail just what such an objective implies in terms of the situations the learners might have to deal with and what they should be able to do by means of language in those situations – what feelings and ideas they would need to express, or ask about, or argue about, and in general conduct personal relations in daily life. It then made recommendations as to the language needed to express functions and notions concerned, whether through the set formulae in which every language abounds, or by the freer use of words in grammatical constructions. What was revolutionary for language teaching, however, was that the apparatus of sentence formation, the grammar and lexicon, were not seen as ends in themselves, but as means to communicative ends. Communicative effectiveness becomes the criterion by which the learners' success (and that of the teaching programme) is to be judged, rather than the error-free performance of formal exercises. The effect was to 'convert language teaching from structure-dominated scholastic sterility into a vital medium for the freer movement of people and ideas' with an emphasis on the use of language in direct person-to-person encounters.

Since 1975, *The Threshold Level* has been used on a large scale by the designers of syllabuses of all kinds: for curricular reform, for examination development, for textbook writing and course design. Functional and notional categorisation has been fully assimilated into the established framework of language learning and teaching. The selection of situations and topics, with the associated specific notions, has stood the test of time reasonably well, as has the framework of general notions and functions less closely tied to particular situations. Over the years, analogous descriptions have been published for Basque, Catalan, Danish, Dutch, Estonian, French, Friulian, Galician, German, Italian, Latvian, Lebanese, Lithuanian, Maltese, Norwegian, Portuguese, Russian, Spanish, Swedish and Welsh. Those for Greek and Irish are approaching completion and work has started on Czech and Hungarian. It is most likely that others will follow. These versions have not been mere translations. In each case the priority objectives have necessarily taken account not only of the semantic categories obligatorily represented in the grammar of the language concerned, but also of the differences in the cultural concept. In addition, the researchers concerned have frequently contributed new ideas to the development of the basic model. *The Threshold Level* is not itself a syllabus but a statement of objectives. Users have invariably adapted it accordingly and have always felt free to use their own judgement, adding and subtracting categories and exponents as they have seen fit.

It was, however, apparent to the Project Group responsible for the Council of Europe Modern Languages Projects 4 and 12 that the existing model for the specification of objectives did not exhaust the objectives which language learners should set themselves. In 1979 it set up a working party to consider an overall model for the specification of language learning objectives more complex than those set out in the threshold level documents, taking into account the development of the individual as a communicator, learner, social subject and person. Working teams were set up, co-ordinated by the Project Adviser. One, co-ordinated by H. Holec, was concerned with the development of the learner as a communicator and as a learner. The second, co-ordinated by D. Coste, was concerned with the personal and social development of the learner. The papers produced were published by the Council of Europe in 1984, together with analytical summaries by the co-ordinators and a 'consolidated report' by the Project Adviser, as *Towards a more comprehensive framework for the definition of language learning objectives*. On the basis of these preliminary studies, J. A. van Ek was commissioned to organise the various elements into an overall model for the specification of language learning objectives, and to consider the nature and educational implications of each of its components. His study: *Objectives for Foreign Language Learning* was published by the Council of Europe in two volumes: Vol. I *Scope* (1986) and Vol. II *Levels* (1987). In Vol. I, Chapter 6, he presents a *Framework for comprehensive foreign language learning objectives* distinguishing the following components:

- communicative ability:
  - linguistic competence
  - sociolinguistic competence
  - discourse competence

- strategic competence
- socio-cultural competence
- social competence
• optimal development of personality:
  - cognitive development
  - affective development

Following the successful completion of Project 12 in 1987, the Council for Cultural Co-operation of the Council of Europe launched a further Project: *Language learning for European citizenship*. Among its priority themes in the area of language learning and teaching methodology was 'revising the original threshold level specification as applied to English to take account of developments in the 15 years since it was conceived as a first pioneering experiment'. A number of institutions concerned with the promotion of English as a foreign language: the British Council, the University of Cambridge Local Examinations Syndicate and BBC English expressed their readiness to support the work of revising and extending both *The Threshold Level* and *Waystage*. We should like to take this opportunity of thanking them warmly for this. Accordingly, the Council of Europe commissioned a thorough revision, which was undertaken in 1989–90 and published as *Threshold Level 1990*. This edition is closely based upon that publication, but the opportunity has been taken to make corrections and to improve the presentation.

We wish here to acknowledge our indebtedness to L. G. Alexander for his contributions to the original specification. It will, however, be seen that the present work is, echoing van Ek's Introduction to the 1986 volume: 'one of the results of many years of intensive collaboration and genuine interaction with colleagues from several European countries brought together in the framework of successive modern language projects of the Council of Europe. The number of those who in some way or other, directly or indirectly, have contributed to our study is so large that we can only say to them, collectively, "Thank you all".'

J. A. van Ek

J. L. M. Trim

Acknowledgement
The Council of Europe wishes to acknowledge the important financial contribution made to this work by the University of Cambridge Local Examinations Syndicate, BBC English and the British Council.

Introduction

1 Target Group

Spread all over the world, there are hundreds of millions of people for whom English is the key that may unlock the door of the space assigned to them by birth and upbringing. A command of this language will enable them to extend their mental horizons beyond almost any geographical or cultural limitations, and, if so desired, also physically to cross the threshold into the world outside. That, in fact, hundreds of millions are prepared to make an effort to this purpose has been shown by the success of the BBC'S multi-media course *Follow Me!*, which in the late 1970s and early 1980s actually attracted such numbers.

It is for this target group that *Threshold Level 1990* has been developed. They will be genuine beginners or so-called 'false beginners' (i.e. those who have acquired some familiarity with the foreign language but feel they need a fresh start). They are interested in acquiring a general basic ability in English even though, individually, each of them may have their own specific needs and wishes and many of them may eventually want to go much further than this basic level. Finally, their motivation is assumed to be practical rather than academic.

2 Criteria

An objective designed for such numbers as referred to above has to be flexible enough to allow of a large variety of concretisations in accordance with the specific circumstances of different groups or individuals. It has to be suitable for utilisation in the design of courses for mass audiences as well as in the development of learning materials tailored to satisfy the needs of small groups or individuals. It has to provide for contacts with native speakers of English as well as with native speakers of other languages who use English as an international medium of communication. And, finally, it has to be manageable within a reasonable time by at least the large majority of those who are prepared to make a genuine effort.

An objective for a target group as large and varied as the one we have in mind is necessarily based on assumptions as to what communicative needs the members of this group are likely to have in common. It cannot, therefore, directly cater for such needs and interests as are shared by only a minority of this group, however large this minority may be. At the same time, it would fall short of its purpose if it did not at least provide a framework in which any expansions required for such sub-groups might be harmoniously accommodated.

3 Adaptability

By way of exemplification we shall consider, in the present section, the relevance of *Threshold Level 1990* to the needs of what is likely to be a substantial sub-group of the overall target population, namely those who will have to use the foreign language particularly for professional purposes. As a general objective *Threshold Level 1990* does not specifically cater for the needs of this sub-group. Yet, the ability to use English for professional purposes is, first and foremost, the ability to use English. In using English for professional purposes, no less than for any other purpose, people will have to be able to ask questions and to provide information, to elicit opinions, views, preferences, and to express them, to refer to past, present and future events, to express reasons why and conditions under which something may come to pass and to understand others doing so, etc. Also, they will have to be familiar with certain social conventions and common assumptions inherent in manners of expression in the English language, and they will need to be aware of how cultural differences may be reflected in communicative behaviour. And then, of course, they will also need experience in coping with the inevitable occurrence of situations which overtax their linguistic or sociocultural resources. All these elements of communicative ability – and many more – are included in *Threshold Level 1990*. Collectively, they constitute the general basic ability which we have attempted to describe and specify in this objective. In our view, this ability is required by all those who wish to use English with a certain measure of confidence in a range of 'normal' communication situations, i.e. in situations for which it is never possible to predict exactly what one will need to be able to say or write and what one will be required to understand. In this respect, then, *Threshold Level 1990* is also an appropriate objective for those who wish to be able to use English particularly for professional purposes. However, it has further potential. Through its comprehensive system of categorisation and the open-endedness of the various specifications it offers virtually unlimited possibilities for such expansions as may serve the purposes of particular sub-groups of the target population. Not only may the various categories be separately expanded, but several of them contain slots for the insertion of further (sets of) elements. Thus, for instance, on behalf of those who wish to learn English particularly for professional purposes, text types of a professional nature may be added to the reading component, the writing component may be expanded as required, the topic specification may be supplemented with further topics of professional interest, and open-ended lists within the topics can be filled in accordance with the needs and interests of particular learner groups.

4 Flexibility

As was also claimed in the previous section, *Threshold Level 1990* has a high degree of internal flexibility. How this flexibility is to be exploited, depends to a large extent on the educational context in which the learning of the foreign language takes place and the effects that this learning is meant to produce. For the learning of a foreign language is an educational experience which may benefit the learners in several different ways. If undertaken as part of an overall educational programme, foreign language learning may, through the contacts it provides with another culture, play an essential role in widening the learners' horizon, in stimulating their awareness of the potential validity of different value systems, of different ways of organising, categorising and expressing experience, etc. If viewed in the perspective of permanent education, a foreign language course may equip the learners with skills and insights that will facilitate the subsequent expansion of their ability in the foreign language or the subsequent learning of one or more other foreign languages. If pursued in a social context, foreign language learning may contribute to the development of the learners' understanding of the complexities of personal interaction; it may prepare them to function more effectively in social contacts, not only in the foreign language but also in their native language, etc.

Many more of the potential benefits of foreign language learning are listed in van Ek, *Objectives for Foreign Language Learning, Vol. 1: Scope*, Strasbourg 1986. Which of these learning effects, and how many of them, are explicitly or implicitly aimed at in a foreign language course, depends on the educational context in which the course is offered and/or taken, as well as on the educational views of those who provide the course and/or of those who take it.

5 What is new in *Threshold Level 1990*

Threshold Level 1990 is designed to fit into a wide variety of educational contexts and to suit a wide variety of learning aims. In this respect it corresponds to its predecessor, *The Threshold Level in a European unit/credit system for modern language learning by adults*, first published by the Council of Europe in 1975. The main difference is that now those

be able, at least for the moment, to let go of that anger.

He also comes into awareness that, in part, he married a controlling person in the first place because of his willingness to live through the feeling of being controlled. Most marriages and relationships have unhealthy dynamics of this kind, and harmony and love can be established when these unhealthy aspects are understood.

The above three basic steps can be described again, this time with a different emphasis: Step 1, during or after a painful emotional difficulty, we recognize the specific emotional attachment that is at the root of our distress, aided if necessary by referring to the three stages of negative emotions described earlier; Step 2, we understand how our emotional distress (and, possibly, our accompanying inappropriate behaviors) can be part of a defense apparatus that tries to cover up our participation in our own suffering (see examples throughout this book of the defenses we employ); and, Step 3, we correlate the results of Step 1 and Step 2 with memories from childhood when we felt similar distress or pain, as we recognize the unconscious choices we now make to continue to circulate such negativity in the present.

This self-knowledge helps us avoid "going negative" in challenging situations. It gives us the power to remain cool, while still responding effectively as the situation requires.

Often times it's not a matter of what we do in challenging situations, but whether or not we "go negative." Suppose you are in grocery store, hurrying to check out. Someone cuts in front of you at the checkout line. You can be aggressive and challenge the person, or you can be passive and say nothing. If you're aggressive, there's a danger of "going negative" and being belligerent. If you go over the line of civil conduct, you'll likely suffer later with feelings of guilt and embarrassment for your excessive or reactive aggression. If you say nothing, you can also "go negative," as you pout and fume and, later, criticize yourself for passively letting the shopper get away with his rudeness.

How do you manage in such a situation not to go negative? You have to be able to take responsibility for your own negativity. Such negativity belongs to you. The other shopper is not causing it; he or she is only triggering it. You need to see the elements of your negativity. Are you feeling disrespected by the other shopper? If that feeling pains you, it means you're likely attached to negative emotions involving feeling unimportant and not valued. This reveals your conflicted relationship with yourself. Are you feeling held up or held back? That's another common emotional attachment, which people are quick to cover up, often with anger.

At the checkout, if you happen to be reacting in anger or suffering in silent misery, you uncover your secret willingness to experience that old, unresolved feeling of being disrespected or devalued (or held back). You see that, unwittingly, you are producing your own suffering. You let go of it by "confronting" your willingness to recycle this old unresolved negative feeling. This is a powerful way to "own" your negativity and to dislodge it.

If you understand your deadly flaw in this manner and are working it out, you're in a stronger position to speak calmly to the other shopper and let this person know, if it's appropriate to do so, that he or she was rude toward you. If this person speaks rudely back to you, you can deflect that aggression rather than absorb it, as you feel satisfied in letting your accusation stand.

When the shopper cuts in front of you, you can also decide to say nothing and either wait patiently, perhaps using the time for productive reflection or a peek at email messages, or you can try another checkout. Your temptation, however, might be to indulge in feelings of being passive or in feelings of being held back or discounted. When you recognize these feelings as your own issues, you can refrain from feeling anger at the other shopper. You can be at peace with yourself, even as you wait five or ten minutes longer at the checkout. You could, for instance, spend the time processing the experience, using your insight to eliminate any painful symptoms.

As we see our own negativity more clearly, we learn to be more detached from the shortcomings and injustices of our world. This doesn't mean we're indifferent to them. We can still respond assertively to injustice, but we don't suffer unnecessarily. We understand that much of the negativity we feel belongs to us. In other words, we're the ones who "go negative." We are "hit up" with this negativity because we don't see clearly enough the operating system that produces it. We can't legitimately blame others for it. That's just a way to cover up our participation in self-suffering and to deny the extent of our own negativity. The way to eliminate it is to get to its source, which is the best way to bring change or reform to ourselves, our family, and to our world.

What could be more of a challenge for human intelligence than to resolve a psychological quirk through which—despite our conscious aspirations to win, to get, to be free and loved—we secretly entertain feelings of losing, not getting, and being helpless and rejected?

The next chapter briefly examines more factors in humankind's reluctance to consider the existence of the deadly flaw. An assortment of evidence is presented to help readers overcome emotional bias against this book's thesis.

components of communicative ability which particularly allow it to be related to a wider educational context are identified and explicitly incorporated into the objective. Thus, *Threshold Level 1990* includes discourse strategies, a sociocultural component, compensation strategies, and a 'learning-to-learn' component. In addition, it contains numerous major and minor improvements in the specification of those categories which were already distinguished in the original *Threshold Level* as well as certain adjustments reflecting differences in assumptions as to foreign language needs in the 1990s as compared to the 1970s. Some of the improvements have been designed to make the specification more accessible. They include re-arrangements in the classification of the language functions, a re-designed grammatical summary and the provision of a subject index. Other changes are of a more fundamental nature, such as the explicit treatment of selected intonation patterns, the addition of two new categories of language functions, 'structuring discourse' and 'communication repair', and the introduction of several open-ended items in the list of specific notions.

Such changes and additions as distinguish *Threshold Level 1990* from its predecessor result from experiences gained in various applications of the original version and from the further development of insights into the nature of communicative ability and implications of this for educational practice. Much of this we owe to the rich literature bearing on 'communicative language learning and teaching' that has been produced in the last 15 years or so. As authors of a new threshold-level version we are particularly indebted to all those who, since the original version for English came out, have undertaken the development of parallel versions for other European languages. Based on the same model, each of these versions bears witness to the application of fresh insights to the specification of communicative objectives.

6 Learning load

Threshold Level 1990 has more components than the old one and in some cases – particularly 'reading' and 'listening' – it requires more of the learners than its predecessor did. At first sight, then, it might seem as if it represents a heavier learning load. It is our assumption, however, that in practice this will not appear to be the case. The new components are largely concerned with the acquisition of strategies and the development of insights and awareness. Their incorporation will have a qualitative rather than a quantitative effect. It does not necessarily increase the number of learning items, but it will affect the presentation and practice of these items. It will involve, for instance, the selection of texts not only for (pragma-)linguistic relevance but also for sociocultural relevance or for relevance with regard to 'coping strategies'. It will also mean that learning tasks will have to be made transparent enough for the learner to understand how the performance of these tasks may contribute to the achievement of his or her aims. The promotion of the development of various types of insight and awareness will require the introduction of teaching/learning procedures which are not yet commonly found in language courses. One such procedure is described in the recently developed 'Stage 3 level' brochure of the International Certificate Conference.[1] It concerns the development of sociolinguistic awareness and appropriate strategies and consists of three steps:

- exposure to a variety of situations in which such features as participant roles, setting, communicative goal, etc., significantly influence the choice of language-forms;

- stimulating awareness of this influence through observation, reflection, discussion;

- involving the learner in similar situations for active practice.

The introduction of such a procedure into a language course, we assume, will make learning more effective rather than more demanding.

No more do higher demands with regard to 'reading' and 'listening' necessarily increase the actual overall learning load. On the contrary: it is increasingly recognised that frequent exposure to texts – or the intensive practice of 'receptive skills' – will contribute substantially to the efficient development of productive ability as well. In fact, what we propose in *Threshold Level 1990* is much more in agreement with current educational practice than the more modest requirements of the original *Threshold Level*.

The increased flexibility of *Threshold Level 1990* makes an assessment of the learning load in terms of 'an average number of learning hours' even more difficult than it used to be. This is particularly due to the inclusion of a fairly large number of open-ended items in the list of topic-related specific notions and to the comparatively low level of specificity in the description of such 'new' components as sociocultural competence, compensation strategies and learning-to-learn. In these cases various concretisations are possible in accordance with the needs and interests of individual learners or groups of learners. The nature of these concretisations may very well affect the weight of the overall learning load and consequently the number of hours required to master it. If pressed to give a general indication,

---

1 *Foreign Languages in Adult and Continuing Education; Specifications for Stage 3 Level of the International Certificate Conference Language Certificate System: English*, third draft, Deutscher Volkshochschul-Verband e.V., Bonn-Frankfurt 1987.

nevertheless, we can only say, at this stage, that we assume the learning load for *Threshold Level 1990* to be similar to that for its predecessor and that there is some evidence that, with adequate guidance, absolute beginners need an average of 375 learning hours – including independent work – to reach the older objectives.

7 Waystage 1990

The estimated learning load for *Threshold Level 1990* may appear to be very formidable indeed, particularly to learners with only little educational experience. Yet, it is our aim to encourage people to learn a foreign language rather than to deter them from doing so. Also, we would not wish to maintain that the achievement of a lower level of communicative ability than *Threshold Level 1990* could not be very much worthwhile to learners. We therefore provide, in a separate publication, a less demanding objective under the name of *Waystage 1990*. *Waystage 1990* has been derived from *Threshold Level 1990*, is based on the same model and contains the same components. It is a coherent objective in its own right, offering the learners a level of ability that may serve many of their language purposes without, however, enabling them to operate in the foreign language with the same measure of freedom as *Threshold Level 1990* is meant to provide. The learning load of *Waystage 1990* is estimated to be about half of that required for *Threshold Level 1990*. For beginning learners who are unable or unwilling to commit themselves right from the start to the expenditure of time and energy required for the higher objective, *Waystage 1990* may be an acceptable alternative. And it is not unreasonable to expect that many of those who have first reached the lower objective may be encouraged by the experience of successful learning to undertake the further learning effort that will take them to *Threshold Level 1990*.

1 The objective: levels of specificity

The objective will be formulated in three stages, or at three levels of specificity:

1 General characterisation

2 Extended characterisation

3 Specification

The *general characterisation* is meant as an overall description for rapid orientation.

The *extended characterisation* is a detailed description for all potentially interested parties, including the learners themselves.

The *specification* is a fully detailed description meant for course designers, curriculum planners, test constructors, etc.

2 The objective: general characterisation

- As temporary visitors to, or temporary residents in, a country where the foreign language is used for general communication purposes,
- when dealing with foreign visitors or temporary residents in their own country, using English as a common means of communication,
- in contact with native or with non-native speakers of the foreign language in another foreign country,
- when encountering written or spoken texts in the foreign language,

the learners will be able to use the foreign language in such a way as to cope with the (principally linguistic) requirements of those situations they are most likely to find themselves in, particularly:

- situations, including practical transactions in everyday life, requiring a largely predictable language use;
- situations involving personal interaction, enabling the learners to establish and to maintain social contacts, including those made in business contacts;
- situations involving indirect communication, requiring the understanding of the gist and/or relevant details of written or spoken texts.

3 The objective: extended characterisation

1   **Learners will be able to cope with transactional situations of everyday life requiring a largely predictable use of language.**

1.1   Contacts with officials

In all contacts with officials learners should be able to ask for repetition, clarification and explanation, etc. of any information, questions or documents not understood, and should be able to ask for the services of an interpreter and/or legal adviser in case of serious difficulty (cf. Chapter 12).

1.1.1   Immigration

Learners should be able to understand and complete necessary documentation.

Learners should be able to understand and answer questions concerning:

- personal identification (cf. Chapter 7, 1.1–1.12)
- the duration and purpose of their visit

1.1.2   Customs officers

Learners should be able to understand and complete necessary documentation.

Learners should be able to understand and answer necessary questions concerning:

- whether they have dutiable items to declare
- the contents of their luggage and the value of items
- where they have come from and where they have acquired items of property
- whether items are for personal use or as gifts or for commercial use

1.1.3   Security officers

Learners should be able to understand and answer questions covering:

- the contents of their hand-baggage
- whether their baggage contains specified items (e.g. electronic equipment, real or toy weapons, etc.)

1.1.4   Police, traffic wardens, etc.

Learners should be able to:

- understand and answer questions concerning:

- personal identification
- details of any vehicle they drive
- details of any property lost or stolen
- their recent actions
- their intentions and reasons for acting

- apologise and ask for understanding of their position in case of minor infringements of regulations

- ask questions and understand the answers given regarding regulations (parking, public access to buildings, etc.)

(See also 1.11 'Finding the way'.)

- summon police assistance in the case of emergency (e.g. an accident, assault, robbery)

1.2 Arrangements for accommodation
(See Specific Notions 2.1–6.)

1.2.1 Accommodation for visitors
Learners should be able to:

- book accommodation by letter or telephone

- enquire about the nature and availability of accommodation in travel agents, or on arrival at a hotel, guest house, camp site, etc.

- complete registration forms

- complain and secure rectification of poor service, malfunctioning equipment, etc.

- complete departure procedures, query bills, etc.

1.2.2 Accommodation for temporary residents
Learners should be able to:

- enquire, in writing or speech, about accommodation to rent, e.g.

  - the number, type and size of rooms

  - the cost (per week, month or year) and terms of letting

  - the charges, services and amenities provided (e.g. local taxes, gas, water, electricity, etc., furniture and household equipment)

  - the arrangements for repairs and maintenance

- make and confirm inventories of contents and their condition

- make arrangements for and supervise household removal

- make arrangements for services, repairs and maintenance as required

- make oral and written complaints to landlord

1.3 Arrangements for meals
Learners should be able to:

- read and understand advertisements of restaurants, menus, etc.
- discuss the relative merits of accommodation, food, prices, waiting time, etc.
- ask for a (particular) table
- order food and drink
- ask and understand answers to questions on the nature and preparation of dishes
- ask for bill, enquire whether service and tax are included
- query and complain of slow service, poor food, overcharging, etc.

1.4 Shopping: buying consumer goods
Learners should be able to:

- read advertisements in newspapers, magazines, etc. for shops and consumer goods
- read for gist simple explanatory documentation on the nature, use and conditions of sale of goods
- read signposting in supermarkets, departmental stores, etc.
- ask whether goods are available and where they are to be found
- discuss the nature and relative merits of particular choices of goods
- negotiate prices and understand conditions of sale
- make payments and if necessary query prices, addition of bills, etc.
- return faulty, inappropriate or unwanted goods and negotiate replacement, refund, etc.

1.5 Using public transport
Learners should be able to:

- read publicised information (e.g. timetables, types and conditions of sale of tickets)
- enquire as to cost, times, routes of journeys
- discuss relative merits of different means of transport and companies (e.g. duration, cost, conditions of travel)
- order, query and pay for tickets (e.g. destination, class of travel, single or return, route, dates), reserve seats, etc.
- enquire as to location of gates/bays/platforms/quays, etc. of planes, buses, trains, ships, etc.

- register luggage for despatch, use left luggage facilities, report loss of or damage to luggage and property

(for temporary residents)

- enquire about the existence of special rates, etc. and their terms and conditions

1.6 Using private transport (car)
Learners should be able to:

- read, query and complete documentation for car hire
- read mandatory and advisory official road signs
- obtain petrol, oil, water, air and services at service stations
- report and secure repair of mechanical faults and breakdowns
- exchange necessary car and insurance details in case of accident

(See also 1.1.4, Contacts with police, traffic warden, etc. and 1.11, Finding the way.)

1.7 Using information services
Learners should be able to:

- make personal and telephone enquiries

1.8 Visiting public places (museums, theatres, stadiums, discos, etc.)
Learners should be able to:

- read publicised guides to tourist attractions, (newspaper entertainment guides, brochures of particular institutions, posters, handbills, etc.)
- enquire about opening times, prices of admission, performance times, position and nature of seats
- book tickets in advance, or purchase at time of admission
- enquire about facilities and amenities (toilets, refreshments, programmes, etc.)

1.9 Using public services
1.9.1 Post office
Learners should be able to:

- read simple published regulations, counter signs, etc. for specific information
- enquire about postage rates, etc. (e.g. first and second class, letters, postcards, destination categories, registered and express post, parcels, telegrams and fax facilities)

- purchase stamps, postal and money orders
- complete customs declarations, registration forms, etc.

1.9.2 Telephone
Learners should be able to:

- read instructions on use of telephone
- consult telephone directories (including yellow pages)
- use telephone directory enquiries

(See also Language Functions 5.21–5.26.)

1.9.3 Bank
Learners should be able to:

- read public notices (especially service tills, currency regulations and exchange rates)
- enquire about exchange rates for notes/travellers' cheques
- enquire about use of cheques, credit cards, etc.

(for temporary residents)

- enquire about, set up and use bank accounts

1.9.4 Medical services
Learners should be able to:

- read notices (e.g. consultation hours, specialisms, signposting of hospital departments, instructions to patients)
- ask for hospital or general practitioner appointment (by telephone)
- explain nature of complaint and answer questions on place and nature of ache or pain and other symptoms
- understand instructions for treatment at the time and subsequently
- obtain medication from pharmacist

1.10 Educational services (for temporary residents)
1.10.1 As students:
learners should be able to:

- read brochures (e.g. of ARELS, British Council and particular teaching institutions and language schools) and follow admission procedures
- understand and use target language as medium of instruction and as language of social interaction in English language classes and among learners during breaks, at mealtimes, etc.
- report and discuss problems relating to learning, teaching, study facilities, social activities, accommodation, canteen meals, etc.

- discuss and enter for examinations
- read examination regulations, rubrics and questions

1.10.2 As parents:
learners should be able to:

- enquire about arrangements/options for the public/private education of their children (e.g. types of school, entry requirements, cost, dates of terms, equipment required)
- make day-to-day arrangements for school attendance
- read simple notes and reports on children's progress
- attend parent/teacher meetings to discuss children's progress

1.11 Finding the way
Learners should be able to:

- read maps (road maps, train, tube and bus networks, and other direction signs and instructions)
- enquire from officials, service station staff or members of the public how to get to certain destinations, where a particular road or railway line leads to, the destination of a bus or train, etc.
- give similar information to others

1.12 Communicating at work
1.12.1 As temporary residents learners should be able to:

- seek work permits, etc. as required
- enquire (e.g. from employment agencies) about the nature, availability and conditions of employment (e.g. job description, pay, hours of work, free time and holidays, length of notice)
- read employment advertisements
- write letters of application and attend interviews giving written or spoken information about own personal data, qualifications and experience and answer questions about them
- understand and follow joining procedures
- understand and ask questions concerning the tasks to be performed on starting work
- understand safety and security regulations and instructions
- report an accident and make an insurance claim
- make use of welfare facilities
- communicate appropriately with superiors, colleagues and subordinates

- participate in the social life of the enterprise or institution (e.g. canteen, sports and social clubs, etc.)

1.12.2 As a member of the host community, a learner should be able to assist an English-speaking (native or non-native) person with the tasks listed above.

1.13 Private hospitality
(See Language functions, socialising.)

A learner should be able:

1.13.1 **as host, to:**

- issue an invitation, written or spoken

- greet and introduce guests

- explain about features of domestic arrangements

- follow social routines and exercise socialising functions

- exchange information and opinions on personal and social themes

- receive or exchange souvenirs or small gifts

- say goodbye to guests and react appropriately to expressions of appreciation

1.13.2 **as guest, to:**

- reply appropriately to accept or decline spoken and written invitations

- exchange greetings with host and other guests, known or newly met, whether introduced or not

- follow social routines and exercise socialising functions

- exchange information and opinions on personal and social themes

- offer flowers or small gifts

- express appreciation of hospitality given

- take leave, making or confirming travel arrangements as required

2   **In the sphere of social interaction the learner has the ability:**

- to exchange information

- to express, and to understand the expression of, opinions, views, attitudes, emotions, wishes

- to agree upon and carry out co-operative actions

The above in relation to topics of personal and of general interest, particularly:

- personal life and circumstances

- living conditions
- trade, profession, occupation
- education
- free-time activities
- travelling, regions, places, sights
- consumer goods, shopping, prices
- eating and drinking
- social relations
- politics, current events
- weather
- languages, language learning, language problems

For details, see Chapter 7, Specific Notions.

3   **The learner can understand the gist and/or relevant details of written and of spoken texts which have the following characteristics:**

- they are relevant to the situations listed under (1) above or to the topics under (2) above
- they have a clear structure, both conceptually and formally
- the information contained in them is exclusively or mainly offered explicitly
- their understanding requires no or only little familiarity with a foreign culture, other than 'general European culture'
- they are produced in an easily accessible form:
  - written texts are clearly printed and, when appropriate, provided with titles, paragraphing, illustrations etc.
  - spoken texts are produced with minimal acoustic distortion, in the standard pronunciation or a close approximation of this, and at a speech rate which is in the lower range of what is normal

4a   **In connection with (1) and (2) above the learner is familiar with relevant social conventions, e.g.**

- *non-linguistic*: physical contact (hand-shaking, kissing, touching, etc.), significant roles of gesture and mime, etc.
- *linguistic*: verbal ways of drawing attention, ways of addressing, choosing degree of formality/informality, turn taking, contact ending, etc., in accordance with normal conventions of politeness. (See Chapter 11.)

b   In connection with (2) the learner is, moreover, familiar with relevant
        social rituals, e.g.

- visiting rituals (appropriate time for arriving, present giving,
  acceptable conversation topics, etc.)

- eating and drinking rituals

- acceptance and refusal rituals

5   In connection with (3) above the learner can use appropriate
        interpretation strategies both as a reader and as a listener, e.g.

- distinguishing main points and secondary points

- distinguishing fact from comment

- identifying relevant information. This may involve determining the
  audience for whom the text was produced and the attitudes and
  communicative intentions of the author, as well as drawing
  inferences from what is explicit in the text

- making use of clues such as titles, illustrations, typographical
  devices (e.g. bolding, italicising, underlining, paragraphing), and, in
  oral texts, such discourse markers as the placing of emphasis,
  structurally relevant pauses, tone of voice, etc.

6   The learner has some familiarity with characteristic features of the
        foreign culture (i.e. the culture of the major, or one of the major,
        countries where the language is used as native language),
        particularly those affecting:

- everyday life

- living conditions

- interpersonal relations

- major values and attitudes

7   The learner can use techniques and strategies for coping with
        demands of situations which go beyond his/her non-linguistic and/or
        linguistic repertoire, e.g.

- engaging a communication partner's co-operation in filling a gap in
  one's know-how

- appealing to tolerance of a foreigner's 'awkwardness', etc.

- strategies for 'getting one's meaning across' in spite of inadequate
  command of the linguistic code

- strategies for deriving meaning from texts in spite of the occurrence
  of unknown elements

- strategies for enlisting the communication partner's help in solving
  communication problems

- using appropriate aids such as dictionaries, word lists, grammars, and other reference materials.

4 The objective: components of the specification

A communicative approach aims to enable the learners to use a foreign language for their own purposes. What these purposes are, depends on the personality, the circumstances, the needs and interests of the learners themselves. They are never fully predictable, but, starting from a particular target group, however heterogeneous it may be, we can make an attempt to identify those things that all of them are at least very likely to need or wish to be able to do in the foreign language. In order to do this in any useful way we have to try and determine in what situations they are most likely to use the foreign language, what roles they will play in these situations, and what matters they are most likely to have to be able to deal with in the foreign language. Determining all this – especially if we want to arrive at a fairly detailed description – is, in a way, a matter of guesswork. However, we can make at least better educated guesses if we make use of our collective experience, our knowledge of the world, and of whatever amount of consensus would appear to have been – explicitly or implicitly – achieved. In fact, the information on this that is available now is by no means negligible. It may be found in numerous studies that have appeared since the *Threshold Level* was originally published, and it is to be found in the choices made in those course materials with a communicative orientation that have been produced in the last 20 years or so. By and large, the assumptions made in the original *Threshold Level* would seem to have been widely upheld, so that the basis for the present specification is a more solid one than for the earlier one. Yet, it should be constantly borne in mind that these assumptions are made with regard to what the members of a very large target group are supposed to have in common and that the undoubtedly considerable individual differences among these members are deliberately left out of account. This is just another way of saying that the *Threshold Level* is a general objective only, and, moreover, one that is never to be regarded as fixed and closed but as something to be used flexibly and creatively.

In the preceding *general characterisation* and particularly in the *extended characterisation* we described the *Threshold Level* objective. The question is now how this may be most usefully specified, how it may be broken down into a coherent set of elements that may serve the purposes of those for whom the specification is meant.

Our starting-point is the situations in which the learners are most likely to find themselves. Each situation will make its own demands on their communicative resources. At the same time, these demands have a lot in common, something which requires what we may regard as general communicative ability. An economical description, then, of what the learners need to be able to do, will specify the components of this general communicative ability plus, for each situation envisaged, the specific ability required to function adequately in it. The general ability, the ability required in most communication situations, will be the subject of by far the greater part of our specification. In fact, there will be only one component that is directly concerned with specific situation-related ability, and – as is to be expected – this will largely be a matter of concrete vocabulary items.

A communicative approach does not consider *knowledge* of the language – however desirable this may be – as an end in itself. Its goal is the ability to *use* language, to *do* with language the kind of things one needs or wants to do with it.

The starting-point of the specification of our objective, then, is a list of the kind of things people may *do* by means of language. These are things such as describing, enquiring, denying, thanking, apologising, expressing feelings, etc. We refer to these things as 'language functions' and we say that in saying, for instance, *'I'm sorry'* people fulfil the language function of apologising or of expressing regret. The first component of our specification is a list of those language functions that the members of our target group are most likely to need to be able to fulfil.

Language functions are not fulfilled in a void, with regard to nothing. If we say *'I'm sorry'*, we apologise for or express regret about *something*, even though we may not mention this explicitly because it is sufficiently clear from the context in which the utterance is produced. If, however, we were to say *'I'm sorry for being late'*, we explicitly refer to a particular concept, the concept of 'lateness'. The concepts that we may refer to while fulfilling language functions will be indicated here as 'notions'. Among the notions we distinguish 'general notions' and 'specific notions'. General notions are such as may be expressed in almost any situation and specific notions are those which are likely to be expressed typically in particular situations only. In most situations the need may arise to refer to time, to place, to quantity or quality, to express relations between entities, etc. The notions involved in this will be listed in our second component as 'general notions'. A notion such as 'timetable', on the other hand, is likely to be expressed only in a situation of people dealing with 'travelling'; the notion of 'potatoes' is most likely to be expressed in connection with 'eating' or with 'agriculture'. Such situation-related or topic-related notions will be listed in our third component, 'specific notions'. In this third component we shall also give general indications as to what people will be supposed to be able to do in each of the situations or with regard to each topic included here. Such indications facilitate and justify the selection of those notions which may be thought particularly relevant to the members of the target group.

Before passing on to other components of our specification we wish to point out that the above distinctions between functions and notions on the one hand and between general notions and specific notions on the other cannot always be made with full consistency. Thus, it may be argued that certain language functions may just as well be interpreted as expressing notions and that for certain notions the choice between 'general' and 'specific' seems to be an arbitrary one. There is no denying that our system of classification has its shortcomings. Yet, it does ensure the fullest possible coverage, and it has fully proved its value for practical purposes.

The breakdown of language use in terms of the fulfilment of certain functions with regard to certain notions may obscure the fact that in actual communication situations these functions are rarely fulfilled in isolation. Usually a communication situation will require the fulfilment of general functions in various combinations and sequences. In general, the predictability of these combinations and sequences is highly limited. Yet, there are certain features and patterns that occur more or less regularly, and some familiarity with them is indispensable for effective communication. A number of these features are included in our list of language functions under 'structuring discourse', and a more general treatment particularly with regard to dialogues will be given in the chapter on 'verbal exchange patterns' (Chapter 8).

One of the differences between the present objective and the original *Threshold Level* is the stronger emphasis on the ability to deal with printed texts and with spoken texts produced by media. This ability is listed as item 3 in the 'extended characterisation'. Because of this stronger emphasis we include in our specification a separate chapter on 'dealing with texts' (Chapter 9).

We also include a short chapter on writing (Chapter 10), because it may be convenient to have a survey of what may be expected of learners at this level, rather than having to collect this from several different parts of the specification.

The fulfilment of language functions and their sequencing will, to a certain extent, be governed by the social conventions which are observed in a particular language community. These conventions are part of the sociocultural context in which the language concerned is used as the medium of communication. This context may have a strong influence on what people express and how they express it. Even at *Threshold Level* some familiarity with this context, or at least awareness of its potential significance, is essential to effective communication. It will be dealt with in a separate chapter of our specification, called 'sociocultural competence' (Chapter 11).

In many real-life communication situations the learners' resources, in terms of knowledge, skills and insights, will fall short of the requirements of these situations. Successful communication will then depend on the learners' skill in coping with these requirements in spite of the inadequacy of their resources. We shall, therefore, include a chapter on 'compensation strategies' in our specification (Chapter 12).

Finally, we shall pay attention to ways in which the experience of learning a foreign language may be exploited in order to benefit the learners *as learners*. Strictly speaking, this falls outside the scope of the objective as described in the 'characterisations'. Yet, it may be assumed that learners who have some awareness of 'how to learn' are likely to 'pass the threshold' more readily than those who have none. We do not consider it out of place, therefore, to add a 'learning-to-learn' component to our specification (Chapter 13).

In the specification of the *Threshold Level* actual language forms (grammatical structures, words, etc.) play only a secondary role. What is required at *Threshold Level* is that learners should be able to *do* certain things in the foreign language, and *how* they do these things is not our prime concern. With regard to this we confine ourselves to an indication – in the chapter 'degree of skill' (Chapter 14) – of certain quality criteria that are relevant to effective communication at this level. Apart from this, the only thing which we feel it is justified to do in this respect is to give some guidance as to how learners might be able to do all the things specified not only effectively but also as economically as possible in terms of the learning load involved. For this reason we add recommended 'exponents' (linguistic realisations) to the various language functions and to the notions. These exponents are not to be mistaken, however, for a prescribed grammar + vocabulary. They may provide useful guidance, they give a concrete indication of the degree of formality/informality envisaged, and they may be used as checklists, but there their role ends. The same remarks apply to the word index and the grammatical summary added to the specification as appendices.

As the exponents will show, the degree of formality/informality recommended for *Threshold Level* learners is fairly neutral. With their limited familiarity with the ways language forms are used in the sociocultural context concerned, learners are well advised, we feel, to avoid extremes both in the direction of formality and in that of informality. If, nevertheless, there should be a need for more marked registers, the appropriate exponents can always be added. In the lists provided exponents are marked Ⓡ. These are exponents that, we think, the learners are very likely to be confronted with by communication partners but that they will hardly be required to produce themselves. Ⓡ thus means that the learners should at least be able to understand these language forms if used by others. The exponents marked Ⓡ have a high degree of predictability. Beyond these, the learners will be confronted with many other language forms, particularly in

connection with item 3 of the 'extended characterisation'. Because of
the low degree of predictability of these forms, no attempt is made to
provide any further guidance in this document. Such an attempt would
also be futile in the light of the emphasis that is placed here on the self-
help strategies that are supposed to give the learner access to texts
containing unknown elements.

5 Language functions

Introduction

In the present specification the language functions – what people *do* by means of language – are listed in six broad categories:

1 imparting and seeking factual information

2 expressing and finding out attitudes

3 getting things done (suasion)

4 socialising

5 structuring discourse

6 communication repair

The second category is by far the most comprehensive and is subdivided as follows:

2.1–2.4	factual: agreement, etc.
2.5–2.14	factual: knowledge, etc.
2.15–2.22	factual: modality
2.23–2.28	volitional
2.29–2.50	emotional
2.51–2.57	moral

The lists of functions under each category heading are the result of a process of selection. The principle of selection has been throughout that the functions selected should meet the most likely and urgent needs of the learners and that together they should not exceed an average learning load of two to three years for courses of average intensity, i.e. two to three hours per week, 35–40 weeks a year.

In many cases more than one way of expressing a given function is suggested. It is, of course, entirely acceptable for learners to decide not to use the full range of alternatives given. They should, however, be able to understand all the options provided when they are used by other people. The symbol ®, for receptive use only, has been used sparingly to indicate that a particular option, though likely to be encountered in contact with native speakers, is felt to be of lower priority in the learners' productive repertoire.

Language functions may be fulfilled directly and indirectly. They are fulfilled directly if an exponent is used in its conventional meaning, i.e.

in the meaning that would normally be assigned to it if it were used in isolation. *'You should go now'* fulfils the function of 'advising others to do something' directly, whereas *'It's getting late'* – in its conventional meaning fulfilling the function of 'reporting' – may serve the same purpose indirectly. The possibilities for the indirect fulfilment of language functions vary in accordance with the situational and the linguistic context of a communicative act. This variation is such that a systematic description and selection on behalf of our objective is not possible. The exponents we propose, therefore, are on the whole those which may be considered to fulfil the functions concerned directly. This does not mean that the indirect fulfilment of language functions should be avoided in course materials designed for *Threshold Level*. On the contrary, an attempt to do so might lead to highly unnatural language use.

Language functions for *Threshold Level* including recommended exponents

1 Imparting and seeking factual information

1.1 Identifying (defining)

1.1.1 (with suitable gesture)
this (one), that (one)
these, those

1.1.2 It is + me, you, him, her, us, them

1.1.3 the + NP/this, that, these, those (+ NP) + *be* + NP
'This is the ˌbedroom.
The ˇ animal over ·there | is my ˌdog.

1.1.4 I, you, he, she, it, we, they + *be* + NP
'He is the ˌowner of the ·restaurant.

1.2 reporting (describing and narrating)

1.2.1 declarative sentences
The 'train has ˌleft.

1.2.2 NP + say, think + complement clause
He ·says the 'shop is ˌshut.

1.3 correcting

1.3.1 As 1.1 and 1.2, with contrastive stress
ˋThis is the ·bedroom.
The ·train ˋhas ·left.

1.3.2 (correcting a positive statement)
(e.g. Vaˈletta is in ˌItaly.)
No (+ tag)
'No it ˇisn't.

1.3.3 negative sentences
Va·letta 'isn't in ˇItaly.

1.3.4 (correcting a negative statement
(e.g. We 'didn't go to ˌLondon.)
Yes (+ tag)
'Yes you ˇ did.

1.3.5 positive statements (with intensifying *do*)
You ˅did ·go to ·London.

1.4 **asking**

1.4.1 (for confirmation)

1.4.1.1 interrogative sentences
'Did you ˌsee him?

1.4.1.2 declarative sentences with high-rising intonation
You 'saw him?

1.4.1.3 statement and question tag
They ˌlost the ·match, | ˌdidn't they?

1.4.2 for information

1.4.2.1 *wh* questions
(time) when?
'When will the ·guests arˌrive?
(place) where?
'Where is my ˌpurse?
(manner) how?
'How do you ·make an ˌomelette?
(degree) how far/much/long hot, etc.?
'How ·far is it to ˌYork?
(reason) why?
'Why did you ·say ˌthat?

1.4.2.2 **Please (can you) tell me + subordinate clause/ + NP**
'Please can you ·tell me the ·way to the ˌstation?

1.4.3 seeking identification
(person) who?
'Who is ˌthat?
(possession) whose + NP?
'Whose ·gloves are ˌthese?
(thing) what? which + NP?
'What is ˌthis?
'Which ˌsuit will you ·wear tonight?
(event) What happened?

1.5 **answering question**

1.5.1 (for confirmation)
Yes, No (+ tag)
ˌYes, | he ˌis.
ˌNo, | he ˌisn't.

1.5.2 (for information)
declarative sentences, clauses, phrases and single words

1.5.2.1 **(time)** ('When will it ˌhappen?)
At '6 p.ˌm.

1.5.2.2 **(place)** ('Where's my ˌbox?)
'On the ˌtable.

1.5.2.3 **(manner)** ('How do you ˌdrive?)
'Not very ˌfast.

1.5.2.4 **(degree)** ('How ˌfar is it?)
'Not very ˌfar.

1.5.2.5 **(reason)** ('Why are you ˌhere?)
(because +) declarative sentence
Be·cause I am a ˌmember.

1.5.3 (seeking identification)
See 1.1.

2 **Expressing and finding out attitudes**

factual: agreement, etc.

2.1 **expressing agreement with a statement**

2.1.1 I ('quite) aˌgree.

2.1.2 'That's ˌright.

2.1.3 'That's corˌrect.

2.1.4 Inˋdeed.

2.1.5 Eˌxactly.

2.1.6 (with a positive statement)
(You ·work 'hard.)

2.1.6.1 **Yes (+ tag)**
ˌYes, | we ˌdo.

2.1.6.2 Of ˌcourse.

2.1.6.3 ˌCertainly.

2.1.6.4 (ˏYes) I ˈthink/beˈlieve ˏso.

2.1.7   (with a negative statement)

2.1.7.1 No (+ tag)
(You ˈcan't ·stop ˇnow.)
ˋNo, | we ˈcan't.

2.1.7.2 Of ˋcourse ·not.

2.1.7.3 ˈCertainly ˏnot.

2.1.7.4 (No) I don'tˇ think so.

2.1.7.5 I beˈlieve ˏnot.

2.2   expressing disagreement with a statement

2.2.1   I ˈdon't aˏgree.

2.2.2   That's ˈnot ˏright.

2.2.3   You are ˋwrong (ˏthere).

2.2.4   (with a positive statement)

2.2.4.1 No (+ tag)
(ˈSpinach is ˋhorrible.) ˈNo it ˏisn't.

2.2.4.2 ˈNot ˏso.

2.2.4.3 ˈCertainly ˏnot.

2.2.4.4 I ˈdon't ˇthink so.

2.2.5   (with a negative statement)

2.2.5.1 Yes (+ tag)
(To·morrow ˈisn't ˇWednesday.)
ˈYes it ˇis.

2.2.5.2 I think (+ positive statement)
I ·think he ˋwill ·come.

2.3   enquiring about agreement and disagreement

2.3.1   statement + question tag
She is ˋFrench, | ˏisn't she?

2.3.2   ˈDon't you agree (+ that clause)?
ˈDon't you a·gree that she is ˏbeautiful?

2.3.3   Do(n't) you think + complement clause
ˈDon't you ·think it's ˏnice?

2.4   denying statements

2.4.1   That ˈisn't ˏtrue.

2.4.2   No (+ negative tag)
(You ˋsaw me ·there.)
ˈNo I ˇdidn't.

2.4.3   Negative sentences (with not, never, nowhere, nobody, nothing, or not + ever, anybody, anywhere, anything)
I ·saw ˏnothing.
I ˈdidn't ·see ˏanything.

factual: knowledge, etc.

2.5   stating whether one knows or does not know a person, thing or fact

2.5.1   I (ˈdon't) ˏknow

2.5.1.1 + complement clause
I ˈknow she ˇleft, | but I ˈdon't ·know ˏwhy (she ·left).

2.5.1.2 + wh (+ clause)

2.5.1.3 + NP
I ˈknow ·Mrs ˋThatcher.

2.6   enquiring whether someone knows or does not know a person, thing or fact

2.6.1   Do you know

2.6.1.1 + complement clause?
ˈDo you ˏknow that she is ·dead?

2.6.1.2 + NP?
ˈDo you ·know ˏKenya?

2.6.1.3 + wh (+ clause)?
ˈDo you ·know where he ˏlives?
ˈDo you ·know ˏwhy he did that?

2.6.2   Have you heard

2.6.2.1 + complement clause?
ˈHave you ·heard that the ˏPresident has ·died?

2.6.2.2 + of + NP?
ˈHave you ·heard of an·opera called 'Die ˏNachtschwalbe'?

2.6.2.3 + *wh* **clause**
'Have you ·heard what
·happened to‚day?

2.6.3   You know

**2.6.3.1 + complement clause, + don't
you?**
You 'know it's ·six o'ᵛclock,
‚don't you?

2.6.3.2 + NP, + don't you?
You ‚know ·Mrs ‚James, |
‚don't you?

2.6.3.4 + *wh* **clause, + don't you?**
You ‚know where he ‚lives, |
‚don't you?

**2.7   stating whether one
remembers or has forgotten a
person, thing or fact or action**

2.7.1   I (don't/can't) remember

2.7.1.1 + VP gerund
I 'don't remember ·saying ᵛthat.

2.7.1.2 + *wh* **clause**
I 'can't re·member ·where
I ·put my ‚handbag.

2.7.1.3 + complement clause
I re'member that he ·gave
it ‚back.

2.7.1.4 + NP
I re'member our ·holiday
in ‚Spain.

2.7.2   I for‚get.

2.7.3   I have(n't) forgotten

2.7.3.1 + to + VPinf
I've for'gotten to ·lock
the ‚door.

2.7.3.2 + NP
I 'haven't for·gotten your
‚birthday.
I have for'gotten my
‚passport.

2.7.3.3 + VP gerund
'I have 'not for·gotten
·climbing ·Mont ‚Blanc.

2.7.3.4 + *wh* **clause**
I've for'gotten where it ᵛis.

**2.8   enquiring whether someone
remembers or has forgotten a
person, thing, fact or action**

2.8.1   Do(n't) you remember?

2.8.2   Do(n/t) you remember

2.8.2.1 + VP gerund
'Don't you re·member coming
‚home ·last ·night?

2.8.2.2 + *wh* **clause**
'Do you re·member where
you ‚left it?

2.8.2.3 + complement clause
'Don't you re·member that
‚James was ·there, | ‚too?

2.8.2.4 + NP
'Do you re·member Ca‚pri?

2.8.3   Have you remembered

2.8.3.1 + to + VPinf
'Have you re·membered to
·feed the ‚cat?

2.8.3.2 + NP
'Have you re·membered her
‚birthday?

**2.9   expressing degrees of
probability**

2.9.1   (certain'ly)
He will 'certainly be ‚there.

2.9.2   probably
'They will 'probably ‚lose, |

2.9.3   possibly
but they may ᵛpossibly ‵win.

2.9.4   (not) (very) likely
It's 'not very ᵛlikely, … |

2.9.5 impossible
... but 'not im͵possible.

2.9.6 NP + *be* + certain/likely + to + VPinf ❸
The mu·seum is 'certain to be ͵closed.

2.9.7 It is certain/probable/likely/ possible/impossible + complement clause
It is 'likely you will ͵pass.

2.9.8 NP will/must/may/can/cannot + VPinf
That ·painting 'cannot be by Pi͵casso.

2.10 enquiring as to degrees of probability

2.10.1 *be* + NP certain/likely + to + VPinf?
'Is the ·story ·likely to be ͵true?

2.10.2 Is it certain/probable/likely possible + complement clause?
'Is it ·likely to ͵rain?

2.10.3 Will/must/may/can + NP + VPinf?
'Can ·oil and ·water ͵mix?

2.10.4 sentences in 2.9 + high rising intonation
The mu·seum is ′certain to be ·closed?

2.11 expressing or denying necessity (including logical deduction)

2.11.1 (not) necessary/necessarily
'Good ͵shoes | are neces'sarily ex͵pensive.

2.11.2 NP + must/cannot + VPinf
People 'must ͵sleep ·sometimes.

2.11.3 NP + need not + inf
'Classical ͵music | 'need ·not be ͵boring.

2.11.4 so/therefore + declarative sentences
'I am ͵thinking | ·therefore 'I ex͵ist.

2.12 enquiring as to necessity (including logical deduction)

2.12.1 necessary/necessarily (in interrogative sentences)
Is 'that neces·sarily ͵so?

2.12.2 must + NP + VPinf?
ˇMust ·things be ·black or ·white?

2.13 expressing degrees of certainty

2.13.1 confident assertion (positive or negative)

2.13.1.1 certainly (in declarative sentences)
She is 'certainly ·over ͵thirty.

2.13.1.2 I am (quite) certain/sure (+ complement clause)
I am 'quite ͵sure | that 'Stalin ·died in ·19·5͵2.

2.13.1.3 declarative sentences with stressed *do, be* or auxiliary
I ͵did ·post the ·letter.

2.13.1.4 declarative sentences (+ tag) (with low falling intonation)
'Ankara is in ͵Turkey, | ͵isn't it?

2.13.1.5 declarative sentences (+ I think/suppose unstressed)
'Rome is in ͵Italy, | I·think.

2.13.1.6 I know + *that* clause
I 'know I·run is in ͵Spain | 'not ͵France.

2.13.1.7 declarative sentence + tag with low falling/high falling intonation
You're ˋPolish, | ˋaren't you?

2.13.2 tentative assertion

2.13.2.1 to seem
The trans·lation 'seems to be cor‚rect.

2.13.2.2 perhaps/maybe (also in declarative sentences)
'Maybe you're ‚right.

2.13.2.3 I 'don't ˅think so.

2.13.2.4 I (don't) think/believe + *that* clause
I ·don't ·think he has 'ever ‚been ·here.

2.13.2.5 I'm not (quite) sure, but + declarative sentence
I'm 'not ·quite ˅sure, | but I 'think he has al·ready ‚gone.

2.13.2.6 declarative sentence + I think (with rising/ falling–rising intonation)
He's ˋFrench, | I ‚think.

2.13.2.7 declarative sentences + tag with low-rising intonation
You're ·coming on ˋThursday, | ‚aren't you?

2.13.3 complete uncertainty

2.13.3.1 I don't know (+ *if* clause/*wh* clause)
I 'don't ·know if he will ‚come.

2.13.3.2 I'm not (at all) sure (+ *if* clause/*wh* clause)
I'm 'not at all ·sure what he ˋwants.

2.13.3.3 I wonder + *if* clause/*wh* clause
I 'wonder why they ·go to ·London by ‚car.

2.14 enquiring about degrees of certainty

2.14.1 Are you (quite) sure (+ *that* clause/*if* clause/*wh* clause
'Are you ·sure the ·food is ‚cooked?

2.14.2 Do you (really) think/believe suppose + *that* clause?
'Do you ·think this is ·real ‚silk?

2.14.3 How sure are you + *that* clause?
How ‚sure are you that ·Basle is in ·Switzerland?

factual: modality

2.15 expressing obligation

2.15.1 NP + have to/must + VPinf
We 'must be ·home before ‚midnight.

2.16 enquiring about obligation

2.16.1 interrogative sentences and *wh* questions corresponding to 2.15
'Must we ·fill in this ˋform ‚now? ˋWhen ·have we to ‚leave?

2.17 expressing ability/inability to do something

2.17.1 NP + can(not) + VPinf
I can under˅stand ·Spanish | but I 'can't ‚speak it ·well.

2.17.2 NP + *be* (not) able to + VPinf
I am 'able to ·ride a ‚horse.

2.17.3 NP + *be* unable to + VPinf
'John is un·able to ‚read ·yet.

2.18 enquiring about ability or inability to do something

2.18.1 interrogative sentences and *wh* questions corresponding to 2.17
'Can you ·speak ‚Spanish? 'Are you ·able to ·ride a ‚horse?

2.19 expressing that something is or is not permitted, or permissible

2.19.1 NP + *be* (not) allowed
'Smoking is al‚lowed.

2.19.2 NP + *be* (not) permitted ❿
Pho'tography is ·not
per,mitted in the ca·thedral.

2.19.3 People/You/can/may/must not + VPinf
You must 'not be ,lazy.

2.19.4 People/You are not supposed to + VPinf
'People are 'not sup·posed
to ·walk on the ,grass.

2.20 enquiring whether something is or is not permitted or permissible (including seeking permission)

2.20.1 Can/may + I/people/one + VPinf?
'May I ·come ,in?

2.20.2 Do you mind (+ *if* clause)?
'Do you ·mind if I ·sit ,down?

2.20.3 Is it all right (+ *if* clause)?
'Is it all ·right if I ,smoke?

2.21 granting permission

2.21.1 ,Yes.

2.21.2 `Certainly.

2.21.3 'Please ,do.

2.21.4 'That's all ,right.

2.21.5 That's ,quite all ·right.

2.21.6 Of ,course.

2.22 withholding permission

2.22.1 ,No.

2.22.2 You ,can't.

2.22.3 I'm a'fraid ,not.

2.22.4 I'm sorry (+ *but* clause)
I'm ˅sorry, | but it's 'too ,late.

2.22.5 It is not allowed/permitted Not + adverbial (now/tonight) here/in this country etc.)
('Can I ,park here?) 'Not until
·6.·30 p,m.

volitional

2.23 expressing wants/desires

2.23.1 I'd like + NP
I'd 'like an ·ice,cream

2.23.2 I'd like + to + VPinf
I'd 'like to ·wash my ,hands.

2.23.3 I want + NP, please
I ·want a 'cup of ,tea, ·please.

2.23.4 I want + to + VPinf, please
I 'want to ·go to the ,toilet,
·please.

2.23.5 (please) may I (+ VPinf)
'Please may I ·have a ,drink.

2.23.6 Can I have + NP (please)
'Can I ·have my ,bill, ·please?

2.24 enquiring about wants/desires

2.24.1 'What would you ,like (to ,do)?

2.24.2 Would you like + NP/ + to + VPinf
'Would you ·like a ,cake?

2.24.3 Do you want + NP/ + to + VPinf
'Do you ·want to ·try the
·suit ,on?

2.25 expressing intentions

2.25.1 NP + *be* + going to + VPinf
I'm 'going to ·buy a ·new ,car.

2.25.2 NP + will + VPinf
I'll ex'plain ,later.

2.25.3 NP + intend(s) to + VPinf
'Ann in·tends to ·go to
A,merica.

2.25.4 NP + *be* thinking of + VP gerund
We are 'thinking of ,driving to
·Turkey.

2.26 enquiring about intentions

2.26.1 interrogative sentences and
wh questions corresponding
to 2.25

2.27 expressing preference

2.27.1 I('d) prefer + NP | to + VPinf
I'd pre'fer to ·go by ˌtrain.

2.27.2 I prefer + NP + to + NP
I pre'fer ˋhockey | to ˌfootball.

2.27.3 I('d) rather (not) + VP
I'd 'rather ·not ˌfly ·there.

2.27.4 I('d) rather VPinf (than + contrastive element)
I'd 'rather ·drink ˌcoffee | than ˌtea.

2.28 enquiring about preference

2.28.1 interrogative sentences and *wh* questions corresponding to 2.27
'Do you pre·fer ˌcoffee to ·tea?
'Which do you preˌfer?
'Where would you ·rather ˌgo, | 'London or ˌOxford?

2.28.2 NP or NP?
'Tea or ˌcoffee?

2.28.3 Adj or Adj?
'Black or ˌwhite?

emotional

2.29 expressing pleasure, happiness

2.29.1 That's ˋlovely/ˋwonderful/ˋgreat!

2.29.2 How ˋnice!

2.29.3 I'm/I feel so ˋhappy!

2.29.4 I'm 'very ˌpleased.

2.29.5 I'm (very) glad/delighted (+ *that* clause to + VPinf)
I'm 'very ·glad to ˌsee you ·here.

2.30 expressing displeasure, unhappiness

2.30.1 'Oh ˌdear!

2.30.2 I 'don't ·feel very/a·t all ˌhappy.

2.30.3 I ·feel/am ·feeling ('very unˌhappy/ˌmiserable.

2.31 enquiring about pleasure/displeasure happiness/unhappiness

2.31.1 'How ˌare you?

2.31.2 'How are you ˌfeeling?

2.31.3 'Are you ˌhappy?

2.31.4 'Are you ˌpleased?

2.32 expressing liking

2.32.1 NP + *be* (very) good/nice/ pleasant
This ·coffee is 'very ˌgood.

2.32.2 I like/enjoy + NP/VP gerund (very much)
I 'like ·riding ·very ˌmuch.

2.32.3 I love NP/VP gerund
I 'love ˌcats.

2.33 expressing dislike

2.33.1 Ugh!

2.33.2 NP + *be* not (very/at all) nice/pleasant
That's ·not aˈt all ˌnice.

2.33.3 NP + *be* + nasty/horrible
'Sour ·milk is ˌnasty.

2.33.4 I don't like/enjoy NP/VP gerund (very much/at all)
I 'don't ˌlike | ˌsweet ·tea.

2.33.5 I hate + NP/VPgerund
I 'hate ˌhurting ·people.

2.33.6 I'd hate/I wouldn't like + to + VPinf
I 'wouldn't ·like to be ˌlate.

2.34 enquiring about likes and dislikes

2.34.1 Do you like/enjoy NP/VP gerund
'Do you en·joy ˌballet?

2.34.2 How do you like NP/VP gerund
'How do you ·like ·playing ‚pop ·music?

2.34.3 'What do you ‚like?

2.35   expressing satisfaction

2.35.1 ˋGood!

2.35.2 ˋFine!

2.35.3 demonstrative + *be* (very) good/nice
·That's ˋgood.

2.35.4 (This is) 'just what I ‚want(ed)/ ‚need/‚meant/·had in ‚mind.

2.35.5 (following dissatisfaction)

2.35.5.1 'That is ‚better.

2.35.5.2 It's ('quite) all ‚right (‚now).

2.35.5.3 'That will ‚do.

2.35.5.4 That is ('good) e‚nough.

2.36   expressing dissatisfaction

2.36.1 declarative sentences
'This ·soup is ‚cold.
The 'T‚V ·doesn't ·work.

2.36.2 I'm not satisfied/happy (with this + NP)
I'm 'not ·happy with this ‚fridge.

2.36.3 I don't like/want this (+ NP)
I 'don't ‚want this ·soup.

2.36.4 I don't like/want NP like this
I 'don't ‚like ·cabbage like ·this.

2.36.5 Demonstrative *be* not right (yet)
This is 'not ‚right ·yet.

2.36.6 Demonstrative *be* not want I want(ed)/had in mind/meant
These are 'not what I ·had in ‚mind.

2.36.7 That will 'not ‚do.

2.36.8 That is 'not ‚good e·nough.

2.37   enquiring about satisfaction/dissatisfaction

2.37.1 Are you satisfied/happy (with + NP)?
'Are you ‚satisfied with your ·meal?

2.37.2 Do you like NP like this?
'Do you ‚like ·coffee like ·this?

2.37.3 ·Is it 'all ‚right (‚now)?

2.37.4 'Is this what you ‚want(ed)/ ‚need/ ‚meant/·had in ‚mind?

2.37.5 How do you like/find NP?
'How do you ·find our ‚beer?

2.37.6 'What is the ‚matter?

2.38   expressing interest

2.38.1 ˋReally!

2.38.2 Is 'that ‚so!

2.38.3 'How ‚interesting!

2.38.4 I am (very) interested in NP/VP gerund
I am 'interested in ·old ‚stamps.

2.38.5 NP interests me (greatly)
'Greek ·men ·interest me ‚greatly.

2.39   expressing lack of interest

2.39.1 'How ‚boring!

2.39.2 I am bored (by NP)
I am ˋbored | by ‚politics | on ·T‚V.

2.39.3 I am not/not very/not at all interested in NP/VP gerund
I am not a't all ‚interested | in ·going a‚broad.

2.39.4 NP does not interest me (very much/at all).
·Sport does 'not ·interest me a‚t all.

2.39.5 It doesn't matter (+ *that* clause/*if* clause)
It 'doesn't ‚matter | if it 'rains or ‚not.

2.39.6 I don't care (+ *that* **clause/** *if* **clause)**
I 'don't ˌcare | if it is 'foggy or ˌfine.

2.39.7 I don't mind (+ *that* **clause/** *if* **clause)**
I 'don't ˌmind | if you ˌsmoke.

2.39.8 Wha'tever you ˌsay/ ˌlike.

2.40 enquiring about interest or lack of interest

2.40.1 Are(n't) you interested in NP/VP gerund?
'Aren't you 'interested in ·foreign ˌlanguages?

2.40.2 Do(es)(n't) NP interest you?
'Does phoˌtography ·interest you?

2.41 expressing surprise

2.41.1 'What a surˌprise!

2.41.2 'How surˌprising!

2.41.3 ˋFancy ˌthat! ®

2.41.4 ˋWell, 'this/'that ˌis a sur·prise!

2.41.5 'That is surˌprising!

2.41.6 I'm surprised (+ *that* **clause/to + VPinf)**
I'm surˋprised | to ˋhear ˌthat.

2.41.7 Fancy + VP gerund ®
'Fancy ·swimming at ˌChristmas.

2.41.8 It surprises me + *that* **clause ®**
It surˌprises me | that the ·dollar is ˋso ˌweak.

2.42 expressing lack of surprise

2.42.1 ˋWell?

2.42.2 'So ˌwhat?

2.42.3 (It is) 'Just as I exˌpected.

2.43 enquiring about surprise

2.43.1 Does 'that surˌprise you?

2.43.2 Is 'this/'that ·what you exˌpected?

2.43.3 'Are you surˌprised (+ *that* clause)
'Are you surˌprised | that I ·came to ˌsee you?

2.44 expressing hope

2.44.1 I ('do) 'hope ˌso.

2.44.2 I ('do) 'hope ˌnot.

2.44.3 I (do) hope + *that* clause.
I 'hope it ·stays ˇfine.

2.44.4 I hope/am hoping + to + VPinf
I 'hope to be·come a ˌdoctor.

2.45 expressing disappointment

2.45.1 What a pity + *that* clause!
'What a ˌpity | that they 'can't have ˌchildren.

2.45.2 That's a ('great) ˌpity!
'What a ˌshame!

2.46 expressing fear

2.46.1 ˋHelp!

2.46.2 I'm ˋfrightened.

2.46.3 I'm afraid (+ *that* clause/ to + VPinf/of + NP)
I'm aˋfraid of ·that ·man.

2.46.4 I'm (rather) worried (about NP)
I'm 'rather ·worried about ˌJoan.

2.47 giving reassurance

2.47.1 'There, ˌthere.

2.47.2 'Don't be a ˌfraid.

2.47.3 'Don't ˌworry.

2.47.4 It's ('quite) ·all ˌright.

2.48 enquiring about fear/worry

2.48.1 Are you afraid/frightened (of NP/VP gerund)?
'Are you a·fraid of the ˌdark?

2.48.2 Are you worried (about NP)?
'Are you ·worried about
your ˌhealth?

2.48.3 Is 'something ˌworrying you?

2.48.4 'Is there ·something on your
ˌmind? ❽

2.49 **expressing gratitude**

2.49.1 ˋThank you ('so ˌmuch/'very
ˌmuch (inˌdeed)

2.49.2 ('Many) ˌthanks!

2.49.3 It/That was ('very/'most) ˌkind/
nice/good of you (to + VPinf)
It was 'most ˌkind of you | to
ˌcall.

2.49.4 I'm very grateful to you (for
NP/VP gerund)
I'm 'very ˌgrateful ·to you |
for ˌtelling me a·bout it.

2.50 **reacting to an expression of
gratitude**

2.50.1 ·Thank ˋyou.

2.50.2 'Not aˌt all.

2.50.3 It's a ˌpleasure.

moral

2.51 **offering an apology**

2.51.1 ˇSorry!

2.51.2 I am ('very) ˌsorry!

2.51.3 I'm 'so ˌsorry.

2.51.4 'Please forˌgive me.

2.51.5 I aˌpologise.

2.51.6 I 'do aˌpologise.

2.51.7 (for disturbing somebody)
I 'beg your ˌpardon.
Exˌcuse me ·please.

2.52 **accepting an apology**

2.52.1 'Not aˌt all.

2.52.2 That's ˋquite ·all ·right.

2.52.3 'That's all ˌright.

2.52.4 It 'doesn't ˌmatter.

2.52.5 It 'doesn't ·matter aˌt all/a ˌbit.

2.52.6 Forˌget it.

2.53 **expressing moral obligation**

2.53.1 NP *be* not supposed to + VPinf
You are 'not sup·posed to
ˌdo that.

2.53.2 NP should (not)/ought (not) to
You 'ought to ·drive more
ˌslowly.

2.54 **expressing approval**

2.54.1 ('very) ˌgood

2.54.2 (That's) ˋfine/'excellent.

2.54.3 'Well ˌdone.

2.55 **expressing disapproval**

2.55.1 Tut-tut (clicks)

2.55.2 That's/it's 'not very ˇgood/
ˇnice.

2.55.3 You 'shouldn't do/have ·done
ˇthat.

2.56 **enquiring about
approval/disapproval**

2.56.1 'How's ˌthis?

2.56.2 'Is ·this all ˌright?

2.56.3 'Do you approve (of + NP/
VP gerund) ❽
'Do you apˌprove | of the
·Welfare ˌState?

2.56.4 What do you think of + NP/
VP gerund?
'What do you ·think of ˌcricket?

2.56.5 How do you find NP/VP
gerund?
'How do you ·find ·living in
ˌEngland?

2.57   expressing regret, sympathy

2.57.1 'What a ˌshame!

2.57.2 **What a pity (+ *that* clause)**
'What a ˌpity | 'Peter ·died
so ˌyoung.

2.57.3 **It's a (great) pity (+ *that* clause)**
It's a 'great ˌpity | he ·left the
ˌparty.

2.57.4 **I'm (so/very) sorry (+ *that*
clause/if clause)**
I'm 'sorry if I ᵛhurt you.

2.57.5 **I'm (so/very) sorry about NP**
I'm so 'very ˌsorry | about your
ˌillness.

2.57.6 **I'm (so/very) sorry to + VPinf**
I'm ˌsorry | to ·hear you
are ·going aˌway.

2.57.7 'Oh ˌdear ...

**3   Deciding on courses of
        action (Šuasion)**

**3.1   suggesting a course of action
        (involving both speaker and
        addressee)**

3.1.1   Let's + VPinf!
'Let's ˌgo!

3.1.2   Shall we + VPinf?
'Shall we ˌdance?

3.1.3   We could + VPinf
We ·could 'go for a ᵛwalk.

**3.1.4   What/How about + NP/VP
        gerund**
'How about ·walking ˌhome?

3.1.5   We might (perhaps) + VPinf
We might per'haps ·go by ᵛtrain.

3.1.6   Why not + VPinf?
'Why not ˌfly there?

3.1.6   Why don't we + VPinf?
'Why don't we ·ask them to
ˌdinner?

3.2   agreeing to a suggestion

3.2.1 ˌYes, ˌlet's.

3.2.2 'Why ˌnot?

3.2.3 (That's a) 'Good iˌdea.

3.2.4 'All ˌright.

**3.3   requesting someone to do
        something**

3.3.1   Please + VP imperative
'Please ·sit ˌdown.

3.3.2   VP imperative + please
'Stop ˌtalking, ·please.

**3.3.3   Would/could you (please) +
        VPinf?**
'Could you ·please ·close
the ˌdoor?

**3.3.4   Would you be so kind as to +
        VPinf**
'Would you be so ·kind as to
ˌwait?

**3.3.5   Kindly + VP imperative +
        (please)**
'Kindly ·make ·less ˌnoise
·please.

3.3.6   Would you mind + VP gerund
'Would you ·mind ·opening
the ˌwindow?

3.3.7   Can I have + NP + VP past
'Can I have my ˌshirt ·washed?

**3.4   advising someone to do
        something**

3.4.1   You should + VPinf
You should 'go to the polˌice.

3.4.2   You ought to + VPinf
You 'ought to be more ˌcareful.

3.4.3   Why don't you + VPinf
'Why don't you ·stop ˌworking
so ·hard?

3.4.4   If I were you, I'd + VPinf
If 'I were ᵛyou | I'd 'phone
him ˌnow.

3.5 **warning others to do something or to refrain from doing something**

3.5.1 VP imperative with falling/rising intonation
Be ˅careful! Look ˅out!

3.5.2 **Don't + VPinf**
Don't ˅cut your·self.

3.5.3 **Mind + NP**
'Mind your ˅head!

3.5.4 declarative sentences with implication
That ·knife is ˅sharp. (Be careful not to cut yourself.)

3.6 **encouraging someone to do something**

3.6.1 '**Come ‚on (+ VP imperative)**
'Come ‚on, | 'keep ‚trying.

3.6.2 **Now then (+ VP imperative)**
'Now ‚then, | 'don't ‚stop.

3.7 **instructing or directing someone to do something**

3.7.1 **You + VP (simple present)**
You ·take a 'freshly ·peeled ‚onion.

3.7.2 imperative sentence
'Mix the ·flour, ·eggs and ·milk to‚gether.

3.7.3 passive sentences (esp. in written instructions)
The 'kit is as‚sembled | by 'bolting the ·parts to‚gether. ℗

3.8 **requesting assistance**

3.8.1 '**Can/'Could you ‚help‚ me, ·please?**

3.9 **offering assistance**

3.9.1 '**Let me ‚help you!**

3.9.2 '**Can I ‚help you?**

3.9.3 '**Can I ·give you a ‚hand?** ℗

3.9.4 '**Can you ‚manage?** ℗

3.10 **inviting someone to do something**

3.10.1 **(How) Would you like to + VPinf?**
'How would you ·like to come ‚sailing?

3.10.2 **What/How about + VP gerund**
'What about a ·nice ‚swim?

3.10.3 **Do + VPinf**
'Do have ·one of ‚mine.

3.10.4 **You must + VPinf**
You 'must ·come to ‚dinner ·with us.

3.11 **accepting an offer or invitation**

3.11.1 '**Yes, ‚please.**

3.11.2 ˋ**Thank you.**

3.11.3 **That will be 'very ‚nice.**

3.11.4 **I'd be glad to + VPinf**
I'd be 'glad to ·come ‚with you.

3.11.5 **With ‚pleasure.**

3.11.6 ‚**Right.**

3.11.7 **I'd ‚like/ˋlove to.**

3.12 **declining an offer or invitation**

3.12.1 '**No ‚thank you.**

3.12.2 **(I'm ˅sorry but) I can't + VPinf**
I'm ˅sorry | but I 'can't ‚come.

3.12.3 **It's very good of you + but clause**
It's very ˅good of you, | but my ‚wife is ·ill.

3.12.4 **Unfortunately I can't + VPinf**
Un˅fortunately | I 'can't ·eat ‚cheese.

3.12.5 I'm afraid I can't + VPinf
I'm a·fraid I 'can't ·leave the
˷dog.

3.13 enquiring whether an offer or invitation is accepted or declined

3.13.1 Will you + VPinf (after all)
'Will you be ˈcoming to
·dinner after ·all?

3.14 asking someone for something

3.14.1 (I'd like) NP + (please)
I'd ·like a 'gin and ˷tonic, ·please.

3.14.2 Can I have + NP, (please)
'Can I ·have a ·piece of ˷cake?

3.14.3 Please may I have + NP
'Please ·may I ·have ˷that ·one?
(See also volitional attitudes 2.23–28.)

4 Socialising

4.1 attracting attention

4.1.1 Ex'cuse ˷me.

4.1.2 'Hal˷lo. (informal)

4.1.3 I ˈsay ... ®

4.2 greeting people

4.2.1 'Hal˷lo.

4.2.2 ·Good ˷morning/after˷noon/ ˷evening (more formal)

4.3 when meeting a friend or acquaintance

4.3.1 'How ˷are you?

4.3.2 'How are you ˷keeping? ®

4.4 replying to a greeting from a friend or acquaintance

4.4.1 if in normal health

4.4.1.1 (I'm) ˈfine ˷thank you. | 'How are ˷you?

4.4.1.2 (I'm) 'very ˷well ·thank you | and 'how are ˷you?

4.4.2 if in poor health, etc.

4.4.2.1 ˇWell, | ˇso-so. | 'How are ˷you?

4.4.3 if recovering from an illness, etc.

4.4.3.1 'Much ˷better, ·thank you. | 'How are ˷you?

4.5 addressing a friend or acquaintance

4.5.1 first name
'Hal˷lo ·John, | 'how are you ˷keeping?

4.6 addressing a stranger

4.6.1 honorific (e.g. Professor, Dr, Mr, Mrs, Miss + family name
'Good ˷morning, ·Mrs ·Jones, | 'how are ˷you to ·day?

4.7 addressing a customer or a member of the general public

4.7.1 formal: Sir/Madam
That will be '35 ˷pounds, Sir.

4.7.2 popular, familiar: Dear/Love ®
'How many do you ˷want, dear?

4.7.3 informal: no address form
'Seventy-five ˷pence, ·please.

4.8 introducing someone to someone else

4.8.1 formal

4.8.1.1 address form + may I introduce + honorific + first name + family name
Pro'fessor ˷Smith, | 'may I intro·duce Dr ·Anthony ˷Browning?

4.8.1.2 address form + I'd like you to meet (+ honorific) + first name + family name
'Mrs Ale˷xander, | I'd 'like you to ·meet ·Jonathan ˷Prior.

4.8.2 informal

4.8.2.1 address form, this is + first name + family name
ˈJohn | ˈthis is ·Jane ˌHargreaves, ˈJane | ˈthis is ·John ˌSmith.

4.8.2.2 first name + meet + first name
ˈJenny, | ˈmeet ˌBill.

4.9 **when being introduced to someone, or when someone is introduced to you**

4.9.1 formal

4.9.1.1 ˈHow do you ˌdo?

4.9.2 informal

4.9.2.1 ˈPleased to ˌmeet you

4.9.2.2 ˈHelˌlo!

4.10 **congratulating someone**

4.10.1 Conˈgratuˌlations!

4.10.2 ˈWell ˌdone!

4.11 **proposing a toast**

4.11.1 ˌCheers!

4.11.2 Your (ˈvery) ·good ˌhealth.

4.11.3 Here's to) + NP
ˈHere's to the ·bride and ˌgroom!

4.12 **taking leave**

4.12.1 formal

4.12.1.1 ˈGood ˌmorning/afterˌnoon/ ˌnight.

4.12.2 informal

4.12.2.1 ˈBye-ˌbye!

4.12.2.2 ˈCheeriˌo. ®

4.12.2.3 (I'll) be ˌseeing you (toˌmorrow/next ˌweek, etc.

4.12.3 if you are not expecting to meet again

4.12.3.1 ˈGood ˌbye.

5 **Structuring discourse**

5.1 opening (See also Language Functions 4.1, 4.2.)

5.1.1 on formal occasions

5.1.1.1 ˈLadies and ˌgentlemen!

5.1.2 as participant in a meeting

5.1.2.1 ˈMr/ˈMadam ˌChairman

5.1.2.2 ˋChair (·person) ®

5.1.3 informal

5.1.3.1 ˌRight!

5.1.3.2 Ahem (sound of clearing one's throat)

5.1.3.3 ˌWell ·now

5.2 **hesitating**

5.2.1 looking for words

5.2.1.1 er ...

5.2.1.2 ... you ·know ...

5.2.1.3 ... now ˈlet me ˌthink

5.2.1.4 ... ˈjust a ˌmoment

5.2.1.5 ... ˈwhat's the ˌword for it?

5.2.1.6 ... ˈHow shall I ˌput it?

5.2.2 (for forgotten name)

5.2.2.1 ... ˌWhat's its/his/her ·name?

5.2.2.2 ... ˌWhat do you ·call it?

5.2.2.3 ... ˌthingumajig ®

5.3 **correcting oneself**

5.3.1 ˌNo ...

5.3.2 ˇSorry ...

5.3.3 I ·mean ...

5.3.4 That's ˈnot (e·xactly) what I ·meant to ˌsay.

5.3.5 ˈLet me ·try/·start aˌgain.

5.3.6 or ·rather ...

5.3.7 ·that is to ·say ...

5.4 introducing a theme

5.4.1 I'd like to say something about + NP
I'd 'like to say ·something about the ·problem of pol‚lution.

5.5 expressing an opinion

5.5.1 As ˅I ·see it | ...
As ˅I see it, | 'terrorists are ‚murderers.

5.5.2 In ˅my o·pinion, | ...
In ˅my opinion, | 'most T.·V. ·programmes are ‚boring.

5.5.3 I ˈthink ...
I 'think we should ‚go now.

5.6 enumerating

5.6.1 in the first place ..., in the second place ... (etc.)
In the ˅first ·place, | 'smoking is ‚bad for you, | in the ˅second ·place, | it 'smells un‚pleasant.

5.6.2 First ..., then ..., then ...
'First ‚order, | 'then ‚eat, | 'then ·pay the ‚bill.

5.6.3 ... and ... and ...
'Mix to‚gether | 'flour and 'milk and ‚eggs.

5.6.4 For one thing ... for another ...
For ˅one ·thing | she is too ‚young, | for a˅nother | she is 'not in‚telligent e·nough for ·this ·job.

5.7 exemplifying

5.7.1 For example ... (written e.g.)

5.7.2 For instance ...

5.7.3 ... and so on (written etc.)

5.8 emphasising

5.8.1 in speech

5.8.1.1 use of stress
That's ˋwonderful!

5.8.1.2 word order
Now ˅this ·picture | I 'like ·very ‚much.

5.8.2 in hand- or type-written texts:

5.8.2.1 use of underlining
He is very unreliable.

5.8.3 in printed texts:

5.8.3.1 use of italics
Cairo is the capital of *Egypt*.

5.8.3.2 use of bolding
This is ***most important.***

5.8.3.3 use of capitals
Do NOT park here.

5.8.4 special phrases:

5.8.4.1 especially
These ·cakes are eˋspecially ·nice.

5.8.4.2 (please) note + *that* clause
'Please ‚note | that we are ‚closed on ·Mondays.

5.8.4.3 it is important + *that* clause (not) to + VPinf
It is imˈportant to ·close the ‚door.

5.8.4.4 Now this is important.

5.8.4.5 I must stress the fact + *that* clause
I must 'stress the ‚fact | that 'fire is ‚dangerous.

5.9 summarising

5.9.1 to ˈsum ‚up ...

5.9.2 in ˅brief ...

5.10 changing the theme

5.10.1 ˈsomething ‚else ...

5.10.2 to ˈchange the ‚subject ...

5.10.3 I'd ˈlike to ·say ·something ‚else.

5.11   asking someone to change the theme

5.11.1 I'd 'like to ·ask you ·something ˏelse.

5.12   asking someone's opinion

5.12.1 'What do ˏyou ·think?

5.12.2 'What is ˏyour o·pinion/·view?

5.12.3 'Where do ˏyou ·stand on ·this ·matter?

5.13   showing that one is following a person's discourse

5.13.1 I ˏsee.

5.13.2 ˏYes/ˏNo.

5.13.3 ˏUh-huh.

5.13.4 ˏReally.

5.13.5 ˏOh.

5.13.5 InˏDeed.

5.14   interrupting

5.14.1 Ex'cuse ˏme.

5.14.2 'May ˏI ·come in ·here?

5.14.3 'May ˏI say ·something?

5.14.4 ˇNo, I'm ˇsorry but ...

5.15   asking someone to be silent

5.15.1 Sh!

5.15.2 ˏQuiet, ·please!

5.16   giving over the floor

5.16.1 'After ˏyou.
(See also Language Functions 2.21.)

5.16.2 By ˏall ·means.

5.17   indicating a wish to continue

5.17.1 'One ˏmoment ·please.

5.17.2 'Just a ˏminute.

5.17.3 'Please ·let me ˏfinish.

5.17.4 'As I was ˏsaying ...

5.18   encouraging someone to continue

5.18.1 ˋDo ·go ˏon.

5.19   indicating that one is coming to an end

5.19.1 ˇFinally, ...

5.19.2 To ˇfinish, | I should 'like to ˏsay ...

5.19.3 In conˇclusion, ...

5.20   closing

5.20.1 at the end of a speech
'Thank you for your atˏtention.

5.20.2 at the end of a conversation

5.20.2.1 Well, it's been 'nice ˏtalking to you.
(See also Language Functions 4.12.)

telephone

5.21   opening

5.21.1 on answering a call

5.21.1.1 telephone number
·Oxford 'five oh ·two ·double ˏone.

5.21.1.2 Hallo (this is +) personal name + speaking
'Halˏlo this is 'Mary ˏSmith ·speaking.

5.21.2 when initiating a call

5.21.2.1 personal name + here
Mar'cel Leˏblanc ˏhere.

5.21.2.2 This is + personal name
This is 'Gunther ˏSchmidt.

5.22   asking for:

5.22.1 a person

5.22.1.1 (Can I speak to) + personal name + please?
'Can I ·speak to ˏGeorge, ·please?

5.22.1.2 Could you put me through to + personal name + please
'Could you ·put me ·through to ·Mr ˏOakham, ·please?

5.22.2 extension

5.22.2.1 extension + number + please
Ex·tension 'one oh ˏsix, ·please.

5.23 asking someone to wait

5.23.1 'Hold the ˏline, ·please.

5.23.2 'Just a ˏmoment, ·please.

5.24 asking whether you are heard and understood

5.24.1 'Are you (·still) ˏthere?

5.24.2 'Can you ˏhear me?

5.25 giving signals that you are hearing and understanding
See Language Functions 5.13.

5.26 announcing new call
I'll 'call ˏback/aˏgain ˏlater/this ˏevening, **etc.**

letters

5.27 opening

5.27.1 if name is known

5.27.1.1 Dear + address form (cf. Language Functions 4.5, 4.6)
Dear Professor Jones.

5.27.2 if name is not known

5.27.2.1 Dear Sir/Madam

5.28 closing

5.28.1 following 5.27.1.1

5.28.1.1 Yours sincerely ...

5.28.1.2 (With) best wishes ...

5.28.1.3 Love (from) ...

5.28.2 following 5.27.2.1
Yours faithfully ...

6 Communication repair
(See also Chapter 12: Compensation Strategies.)

6.1 signalling non-understanding

6.1.1 ˅Sorry, I 'don't underˏstand.

6.2 asking for repetition of sentence

6.2.1 (I 'beg your) ʹpardon?

6.2.2 ʹWhat did you ·say ·please?

6.2.3 (˅Sorry) 'could you ·say that aˏgain (·please)?

6.2.4 'Could you reˏpeat that ·please?

6.3 asking for a repetition of a word or phrase

6.3.1 (sorry +) *wh* question
˅Sorry, 'where does she ·live?

6.3.2 (sorry +) *wh* did you say + interrogative clause
˅Sorry, 'what did you ·say his ·name was?

6.4 asking for confirmation of text

6.4.1 Did you say: X?
'Did you say ˏanchovies?

6.5 asking for confirmation or understanding

6.5.1 Do you mean to say + *that* clause?
'Do you ·mean to ·say that they ·aren't ˏcoming?

6.6 asking for clarification

6.6.1 (Sorry) What does X mean?
'What does ˏanglophile ·mean?

6.6.2 What do you mean by X?
'What do you ·mean by ˏgood?

6.6.3 What is X?
'What is ·kicking the
ˌbucket?

**6.6.4 'Could you exˌplain that,
·please?**

**6.7 asking someone to spell
something**

6.7.1 'Could you ˌspell that, ·please?

**6.7.2 'How do you ˌspell that,
·please?**

**6.8 asking for something to be
written down**

**6.8.1 'Could you ·write that ˌdown
for me, ·please?**

**6.9 expressing ignorance of a
word or expression**
(See also Language Functions
5.2.)

6.9.1 I 'don't ·know ·how to ˌsay it.

**6.9.2 I 'don't ·know ·what you ˌcall
it.**

**6.9.3 I 'don't ˌknow the ·word in
·English.**

6.9.4 In (native language) we say …
In ⱽGerman we ·say
Verˌdienst ·Kreuz.

6.10 appealing for assistance

**6.10.1 What is the English for +
(native language word)?**
'What is the ·English for ˌfunghi?

**6.10.2 What is (native language
word) in English?**
'What is framboise in ˌEnglish?

**6.10.3 How do you say (native
language word) in English?**
'How do you say ·hasta
la ·vista in ˌEnglish?

6.10.4 … What do you call it?

6.10.5 … you know …
It's a … 'you ·know …

6.10.6 … er …
I ·found a … er … er …

**6.11 asking someone to speak
more slowly**

**6.11.1 ('Can you ·speak) 'more ˌslowly,
·please.**

6.11.2 'Not so ˌfast, ·please.

6.12 paraphrasing

**6.12.1 a/some kind/sort of + generic
term**
'some ·kind of ˌanimal

6.12.2 something like + related term
'something ·like a ˌcabbage

**6.12.3 something/generic term +
relative clause**
'something you ·make with
ˌeggs

6.13 repeating what one has said

6.13.1 X (simply repeated as spoken)
They'll ·come at '5 oˌ'clock.

**6.13.2 X (repeated more slowly
and without phonetic
reduction)**

6.13.3 I said X
I ·said 'seven ˌhundred.

6.13.4 What I said was X
'What I ·said ˌwas: 'Don't
·walk on the ˌgrass.

**6.13.5 I said that + indirect speech
form or close paraphrase ®**
I ·said that I was 'very ˌtired.

**6.14 asking if you have been
understood**

6.14.1 'Is that ˌclear (·now)?

6.14.2 'Do you underˌstand (·now)?

6.15 spelling out a word or expression

6.15.1 spelling out English letter names
M- O- N- K- E- Y- S

6.15.2 X is spelt: ...
Tough is spelt T- O- U- G- H.

6.15.3 You spell it: ...
You spell it B- R- I- G- H- T.

6.16 supplying a word or expression

6.16.1 Do you mean X?
'Do you ·mean ,mushroom?

6.16.2 Perhaps you mean X?
Per'haps you ·mean ,raspberry?

6.16.3 I think you mean X?
I 'think you ·mean a ,badge.

6.16.4 X (perhaps)?
,Service ·Cross per·haps?

6 General notions

Introduction

The list of general notions is derived from a consideration of what, in general, people deal with by means of language, of what concepts they may be likely to refer to whatever the specific features of a particular communication situation may be.

We present the general notions under eight headings:

1 existential

2 spatial

3 temporal

4 quantitative

5 qualitative

6 mental

7 relational

8 deixis

The following list indicates the sub-classes of the notions selected and presents the various notions in the form of their exponents. Strictly speaking, we should have presented each notion and its exponent(s) separately, but since the large majority of the notions would then have to be referred to by means of the corresponding exponent – the lexical item *among* is the exponent of the notion *among* – this would have led to almost constant duplication without any practical gain.

General notions for *Threshold Level* including recommended exponents

1 Existential

1.1 *existence, non-existence*
There is + NP
There's no + NP
There isn't any + NP
the verbs to exist, to become,
to make (as in: She 'made a
·new ˌdress.)

1.2 *presence, absence*
here, not here, there, not there, away

1.3 *availability, non availability*
to have (got)
There is + NP
There's no + NP
There isn't any + NP

ready (as in 'When will it be ˌready?)

1.4 *occurrence, non-occurrence*
to happen

2 Spatial

2.1 *location*
the following adverbs: **here, there, everywhere, somewhere, nowhere, (not) anywhere, where?; inside, outside (in) the east/north/south/west**
to have been to (as in: She has ·been to ˋParis.)
this, that, these those

2.2 *relative position*
the following prepositions of position:
above ®, against, among ®, at, at the end of, at the side of, before ®, behind, below ®, beside ®, between, in, in front of, inside ®, in the centre of, next to, on, opposite, outside, over, round, under, where + sub-clause ®

2.3 *distance*
distance (as in: The 'distance from ·A to ˌB | is 'five ˌmiles.)
far (away) from, near, in the neighbourhood (of) ®, ... away (as in: It is 'two ˌmiles away.)

2.4 *motion*
the following verbs of motion: **to arrive, to come, to come along ®, to come + to NP** (as in: He 'came to the ˌhouse.), **to fall, to get up, to go, to hurry, to leave** (as in: We have to ˌleave ·now.), **to lie down, to start, to move** (as in: The ·car 'did not ˌmove.), **to pass** (as in: You 'pass the ˌrailway ·station.), **to run, to stand still ®, to stop** (as in: The 'train ˌstopped.), **to walk**

2.5 *direction*
direction
In 'which di·rection is ˌSlough?
the following adverbs: **away, back, down** (as in: 'Are you ·going ˌdown?), **in, out, (to the) left, (to the) right, straight on, up** (as in: 'Are you ·going ˌup?), **east** (as in: He ·went ˌeast.), **north, south, west**
the following prepositions: **across ®, along, down ®, for ®** (as in: He is 'leaving for ˌRome.), **from, into, off, past, through, to, towards ®, up ®, away from**
the following verbs: **to bring, to carry, to follow, to pull, to push, to put** (as in: 'May I put my ·coat ˌhere?), **to send, to take** (as in: I'll 'take it to your ˌroom.), **to take away, to turn** (as in: 'Turn ·left at the ˌriver.)

2.6 *origin*
from (as in: We ·came from ˌLondon.), **out of**

2.7 *arrangement*
after (as in: 'B comes ·after ˌA.), **before** (as in: 'A ·comes before ˌB.), **between, among, first** (as in: 'John ·came ˌfirst.), **last** (as in: 'Peter ·came ˌlast.)

2.8 *dimension*

2.8.1 size
size (as in: 'What ·size ˌshoes do you ·take?)
the following adjectives: **big, deep, high, large ®, low, narrow ®, short, small, tall, thick, thin, wide**

2.8.2 length
centimetre, foot, inch, kilometre, metre, mile, millimetre, yard

long (as in: 'How ˌlong is it?),
short

2.8.3 pressure
heavy, light (as in: I ·want a
'light ˌblanket.), **high, low**

2.8.4 weight
to weigh ⓡ
weight
**gram(me)s, kilo, lbs., oz.,
ton(ne)**
the adjectives light and heavy

2.8.5 volume
gallon, litre, pint

2.8.6 space
big, small
room (as in: You ·have 'plenty of
ˌroom ·here.)

2.8.7 temperature
temperature (as in: The
·temperature is 'too ˌhigh | for
ˌme.), **degree, zero** (as in: It's
'ten degrees below ˌzero.)
**cold, cool, hot, warm
to boil, to burn, to freeze,
(to)heat, to get cold/hot/warm**

3   Temporal

3.1 *points of time*
**(three) o'clock
(five) to/past (three)
a quarter to/past (three)
(sixteen) minutes to/past
(three)
half past (three)
(3) a.m./p.m.** ⓡ
noon ⓡ**, midnight** ⓡ
**1500 (fifteen hundred), 1518
(fifteen eighteen)
at ...**

3.2 *divisions of time*
**moment, second, minute,
quarter of an hour, half (an)
hour, hour, day, week,**

fortnight ⓡ**, month, year,
century
season, autumn, spring,
summer, winter
afternoon, evening, morning,
night, weekend, holiday(s)
the names of days of the
week, names of months**

3.3 *indications of time*
time (as in: 'What ˌtime is it?)
now, then, when?, soon, ago (as
in: 'two ·days aˌgo)
**today, tomorrow, yesterday,
the day before yesterday, the
day after tomorrow
this morning/afternoon/
evening/week/month/year,
tonight last/next + week/
month/year**
prepositions: at (as in: at
'three o'ˌclock, at 'twenty ˌpast
(three), at ˌmidnight), **by** ⓡ
(as in: by 'three o'ˌclock), **in**
(as in: in 'three ˌdays, in a
ˌweek, in ˌsummer, in the
ˌautumn, in '198ˌ9), **on** (as in: on
ˌSunday, on the 'first of ˌJune)
**dates: (spoken) the first of
June
(written) 1 June 1989
Christmas, Easter**

3.4 *duration*
prepositions: during ⓡ (as in:
'during the ˌholidays), **for** (as
in: for 'three ˌhours), **since** (as
in: since '194ˌ5), **till, until** ⓡ**,
not ... till** (as in: He 'won't be
ˌhere | till 'three o'ˌclock.)
to last (as in: It ·lasts 'three
ˌhours.), **to take** (as in: It ·takes
'three ˌhours.)
adjectives: long (as in: a 'long
ˌtime), **short** (as in: a 'short
ˌtime), **quick** (as in: a 'quick
ˌmeal)

3.5 *earliness*
early (as in: You are ˋearly;
There's an 'early ·train on
ˌMondays.)

3.6 *lateness*
late (as in: We'll ·have to
ˋhurry, | we are ˋlate; We were
'too ·late for the ˌtrain; We ·went
to the ˌlate ·show.)

3.7 *anteriority*
present perfect (as in: I
'haven't ˋseen ·John | ˌyet; I've
·been to ˌParis.)
past perfect (as in: I 'hadn't
ˌdone it.)
before + NP/sub-clause
before (as in: I'd 'never ˌdone it
before.)
already (as in: I have al'ready
ˌdone it.)
yet (as in: 'Has he ˌcome ·yet?:
He 'hasn't ˌcome ·yet.)
earlier than ...

3.8 *posteriority*
after + NP/sub-clause
afterwards, later (on)
later than ...

3.9 *sequence*
first (as in: 'First we ·went to
Maˌdrid.), **then** (as in: 'First we
·went to Maˌdrid, | 'then we
·travelled to Gibˌraltar.), **next ❿**
(as in: 'What did you ·do ˌnext?),
finally (as in: ˅Finally | we ·went
ˌback.), **later on ❿, in the end ❿,
afterwards**

3.10 *simultaneousness*
**when + sub-clause ❿, while +
sub-clause ❿, as soon as + sub-
clause ❿**
at the same time

3.11 *future reference*
NP + be going to ...
NP + will ...

**present continuous of verbs of
motion**
**simple present (with
adverbials of future time)**
(as in: We 'leave at ˌmidnight.)

soon
in (as in: in 'four ˌweeks)
**next week/month/year/Sunday,
etc.**
**tonight, tomorrow, the day
after tomorrow, this afternoon**

3.12 *present reference*
present continuous
simple present
present perfect
at present, now, today, still,
(as in: He is 'still ˌworking.)
**this morning/afternoon/year
etc.**

3.13 *past reference*
past continuous
simple past
**yesterday, the day before
yesterday, formerly, just,
recently ❿, lately ❿, last
week/month, etc.**

3.14 *reference without time focus*
simple present (as in:
'Edinburgh is in ˌScotland.)

3.15 *delay*
later (as in: The 'train will
come ˌlater.)
delay ❿ (as in: There will
be a deˌlay.)
to be delayed ❿ (as in: The
'train will be deˌlayed.)

3.16 *speed*
fast, slow
... miles/kilometres per hour

3.17 *frequency*
**always, (hardly) ever, never,
(not) often, once, rarely,
seldom ❿, sometimes, twice,**

usually
daily ®, weekly ®, monthly ®
(as in: There are 'daily ˌflights.)
once every day ®
... times a/per week/month, etc.
on weekdays/Sundays, etc.
every week/Sunday, etc.

3.18 *continuity*
present continuous
past continuous
present perfect (as in: I've
'lived ·here for ·two ˌyears.)
to go on (as in: It will ·go on
for 'five ˌyears.)

3.19 *intermittence*
not always, sometimes, on and
off

3.20 *permanence*
always, for ever, for good

3.21 *temporariness*
for + NP (as in: You can 'have
my ·car for a ˌweek.)
not always
present continuous
past continuous (as in: He
is/was ·living in 'Scotland for
·some ·months.)

3.22 *repetitiousness*
again, many times, twice,
several times ®, again and
again ®

3.23 *uniqueness*
(only) once

3.24 *commencement*
to begin ®, to start (as in: The
'game ·started at ˌseven; He
'started to ˌspeak.)
to go ... (as in: 'Let's ·go
ˌsailing.)
since (as in: I've ·been here
since '7 a.ˌm.), **from (as in:** I
·work from '9 to ˌ12.)

3.25 *cessation*
to end ®, to finish ®, to stop
(as in: The ·game will 'stop
at ˌsix; He 'stopped ˌtalking.)
till, until ®, to (as in: from '9 to
ˌ12)

3.26 *stability*
to remain ® (as in: 'How ·long
will you re·main ˌhere; 'Will it
re·main ˌdry today?), **to stay (as**
in: I will 'stay here for a ˌweek; It
'won't ·stay ·dry for ˇlong.), **to**
keep (as in: 'How ·long will this
·milk ·keep ˌfresh?), **to wait (as**
in: We ·had to ·wait ·only 'five
ˌminutes.)

3.27 *change, transition*
to become (as in: 'Sugar has
become exˌpensive.), **to change,**
to get ® (as in: He's ·getting
ˌold.), **to turn (as in:** The ·leaves
·turned ˌyellow.)
suddenly ...

4   Quantitative

4.1 *number*
singular/plural
cardinal numerals
ordinal numerals
another (as in: 'May I have
a·nother ·cup of ˌtea, ·please?),
about (as in: I have about ˌ£25.)

4.2 *quantity*
the following determiners: **all,**
a lot of, any (also: hardly any,
not any), both, each, enough,
(a) few, (a) little, many, more,
most, much, no, several, some
half (as in: 'Give me ˌhalf of
it; 'Give me the ˌother ·half;
'Give me ·half a ˌbottle.)
at least (as in: I ·need at 'least
ˌ£5.)

a bottle/box/cup/glass, packet/
piece, etc. of ...
See further General Notions
2.8.

4.3 *degree*
comparative and superlative
degrees of adjectives and
adverbs
enough (as in: 'good e‚nough),
too ..., very ...
a bit (as in: a 'bit ‚better; a
'bit ‚tired) ®, **a little** (as
in: a 'little ‚better; a ·little
‚tired), **a lot** (as in: a 'lot
‚better) ®, **much** (as in: 'much
‚better), **almost, hardly** ®,
quite (as in: 'quite ‚old),
rather (as in: 'rather ‚old), **so**
(as in: I'm 'so ‚sorry!)
such ® (as in: It was 'such
`fun! He is 'such a `nice ·boy!)
even (as in: I've 'even ·paid
`£5.)

5 Qualitative

5.1 *physical*

5.1.1 shape
adjectives: **round, square**

5.1.2 dimension
See General Notions 2.8.

5.1.3 moisture, humidity
**dry, wet, damp, moist
to dry, to (make) wet**

5.1.4 visibility, sight
**NP + can(not) see + NP
NP + can(not) be seen** ®
to look (as in: 'Don't ·look
`now!), **to look at, to watch**
adjectives: **dark, light,
(in)visible**

5.1.5 audibility, hearing
**NP + can(not) hear + NP
NP + can(not) be heard** ®

to listen, to listen to
nouns: **noise, silence** ®, **sound**
adjectives: **loud, silent** ®, **soft,
quiet**

5.1.6 taste
to taste (as in: 'How does your
‚soup ·taste?; 'Would you ·like to
·taste ‚this?)
taste (as in: I 'don't ·like the
‚taste.)
adjectives: **bad, nice, bitter,
salt(y), sour, sweet**

5.1.7 smell
to smell (of) (as in: The 'food
·smells `good; 'Can you ·smell
‚gas?; It ·smells of ‚paint.)
smell (as in: The ·flower has a
'nice ‚smell.), **odour** ®,
perfume ®
adjectives: **bad, nice,
pleasant, unpleasant**

5.1.8 texture
adjectives: **hard, rough,
smooth** ®, **soft, strong,
weak** ®

5.1.9 colour
colour
adjectives: **blue, black, brown,
green, grey, orange, red, white,
yellow; light** (as in: a ‚light
·colour; 'light ‚blue), **bright,
dull, dark** (as in: a ‚dark ·colour;
'dark ‚blue)

5.1.10 age
age ®
**I am ... (years old)
How old are you (is he/she,
etc.)?**
adjectives: **new, old, young**
nouns: **adult, baby, child**
month (as in: Her ·baby is 'six
·months ‚old.), **year**

5.1.11 physical condition
adjectives: **alive, all right,**

better (as in: He ·got ˌbetter.),
dead, ill, well
in/out of order ❽ (as in: The
'telephone is ·out of ˌorder.)
to look (as in: You ·look 'very
ˌwell.)
to break, to cut (as in: I've
'cut my ˌfinger.), to (be) hurt,
to die, to fasten, to tie, to
repair, to put right

5.1.12 accessibility
to close (as in: The 'shop
·closes at ˌsix.)
to get at, to open, to reach
adjectives: closed, open

5.1.13 cleanness
to clean, to wash, (to) dust ❽,
(to) polish ❽
adjectives: clean, dirty

5.1.14 material
nouns and adjectives:
cotton ❽, glass, leather,
metal, nylon, paper, plastic,
silk, silver
nouns: wood, wool
made of wood, wooden ❽,
made of wool, woollen ❽
material

5.1.15 genuineness
real (as in: 'Is this ˌreal
·leather?)

5.1.16 fullness
adjectives: empty, full (of)
to fill

5.2 *evaluative*

5.2.1 value, price
How much + *be* ... ? (as in:
'How ·much are ·these ˌshoes?)
to cost ❽
noun: price
adjectives: cheap,
(in)expensive, high, low

5.2.2 quality

noun: quality
adjectives: bad, worse, worst
poor
good, better, best; excellent,
fine, nice
adverb: well (as in: He can
·write ·English ·very ˌwell.)

5.2.3 rightness, wrongness
NP + should (not) + VPinf
NP + ought to + VPinf
adjectives: right, wrong

5.2.4 acceptability, unacceptability
That's all right.
That's fine/nice.
I don't like it.
I cannot accept ... ❽
I'm against ... ❽

5.2.5 adequacy, inadequacy
NP + *be* all right
NP + *be* (not) enough
That will do. ❽

5.2.6 desirability, undesirability
to like
See also Language Functions
2.32–2.36.

5.2.7 correctness, incorrectness
adjectives: better, correct ❽,
incorrect ❽, false ❽, right, true,
wrong, OK
to be right, to be wrong, to put
something right, to make
something better

5.2.8 successfulness,
unsuccessfulness
to fail, to succeed, to try
failure, success
(un-)successful ❽

5.2.9 utility, inutility
(not) useful, useless ❽
NP + can(not) use ...

5.2.10 capacity, incapacity
NP + can(not) ...
NP + will/won't ...
NP + *be* able to ...

5.2.11 importance, unimportance
(not) important, unimportant ®

5.2.12 normality, abnormality
normal, strange, ordinary ®

5.2.13 facility, difficulty
easy, difficult, hard ® (as
in: His ·English is 'hard to
under‚stand.)
difficulty ®

6 Mental

6.1 *reflection*
to believe, to be sure, to be
certain ®, to hope, to know,
to remember, to think, to
wonder ®
no doubt ®
See also Language Functions
2.5–2.8, 2.13–2.14.

6.2 *expression*
to answer, to apologise ®, to
ask, to forbid ®, to invite ®, to
laugh, to recommend ®, to
request ® (as in: ·Guests are
re·quested to 'leave their ·keys at
the ‚desk.), to say, to speak, to
talk, to tell, to thank, to write
nouns: answer, question,
statement

7 Relational

7.1 *spatial relations*
See General Notions 2.2, 2.3,
2.5, 2.6, 2.7.

7.2 *temporal relations*
See General Notions 3.4–3.14.

7.3 *action/event relations*

7.3.1 agency
agent as subject
agent in by adjunct (passive) ®
agent in emphatic: It was X
who ... ®

7.3.2 objective/factitive
objective as object (as in:
'John ·opened the ‚door.)
objective as subject of
passive ® (as in: The 'door was
·opened by ‚John.)
factitive as object (as in: She
·made a 'new ‚dress.)
factitive as subject of
passive ® (as in: 'This ca‚thedral
| was ·built in the 'thirteenth
‚century.)

7.3.3 dative
dative as indirect object (as
in: He 'gave me a ‚book.)
dative in *to* adjunct (as in: He
'gave the ·ticket to my ‚brother.)
dative as subject of passive ®
(as in: He was ·given a ‚book.)

7.3.4 instrumental
instrumental in *with* adjunct
(as in: You can 'open the ·door
with ·this ‚key.)

7.3.5 benefactive
benefactive in *for* adjunct (as
in: I have 'bought this for my
‚wife.)

7.3.6 causative
to have (as in: 'Can I have my
‚shirt ·washed, ·please?)

7.3.7 place
See General Notions, Section
2.

7.3.8 time
See General Notions, Section 3.

7.3.9 manner, means
in this way, like this ®
by means of ... ®
by + Ving
as ® (as in: They 'use it as a
‚fork.)
adverbs: badly, fast, hard (as
in: We ·have to ·work 'very
‚hard.), how?, quickly, slowly,
well

7.4	*contrastive relations*

7.4.1 equality, inequality
(not) the same (thing) (as ...)
to differ ®
difference ®
different (from), else (as in:
'Anything ˏelse?), **other,**
another (as in: 'Give me
aˏnother (=**different**) ·book.)

7.4.2 correspondence
in addition to the exponents
of 7.4.1: **like** (as in: It's ·like an
ˋorange.)
comparative degree + than (as
in: 'John is ˏolder than his
·brother; 'John ·works ˏharder
than his ·brother.)
superlative degree (as in: He
is the 'tallest ·boy in the ˏclass.)
as ... as ® (as in: He is as 'big as
his ˏbrother.)
not so ... as ® (as in: He is 'not so
ˏbig as his ·brother.)

7.5	*possessive relations*

7.5.1 ownership, possession
**possessive adjectives (my,
your,** etc.)
**possessive pronouns (mine,
yours,** etc.)® (as in: 'This is
ˏmine.; as subject (as in: 'Mine is
ˏbetter.)
**genitive singular of personal
nouns**
of adjuncts
with adjuncts, *without*
adjuncts
(as in: You 'cannot ·travel here
without a ˏpassport.)
to belong to ... ®, **to have
(got)** (as in: I have (·got) a
ˎsmall ˏcar.), **to get** (as in: I ·got
a 'nice ˏpresent from him.),
to give, to keep (as in: 'May I
ˏkeep this?), **to own** ®, **owner** ®,
own (as in: This is my 'own
ˏbook.)

7.6	*logical relations*

7.6.1 conjunction
and, as well as ®, **but, also, too**
(as in: ˏJohn is ·leaving | ˏtoo.),
not ... either (as in: ˋI cannot
·swim | ˋeither.)
together
pair (as in: I 'want to ·buy a ·pair
of ˏshoes.), **group** (as in: a
'group of ˏfriends)

7.6.2 disjunction
or

7.6.3 inclusion/exclusion
with (as in: We are 'going to
·take him ˏwith us.), **without** (as
in: We are 'not ·going withˏout
him.)
except ® (as in: We 'all ·went,
except ˏJohn.)
also, too (as in: ˋJohn is
leaving | ˋtoo.)

7.6.4 cause
Why ...?
**because + sub-clause, as +
sub-clause** ®

7.6.5 effect
then ... , so ... (as in: He ˏate too
·much, | so he 'did not ·feel
ˏwell.), **so ... that** ® (as in: He ate
'so ˏmuch | that he 'fell ˏill.)
the re'sult ˏis ... ®

7.6.6 reason
Why ...?
because + sub-clause
since + sub-clause
the reason is ... ®

7.6.7 purpose
to ... (as in: He 'came to ˏhelp
me.)
in order to ... ®
the purpose is ... ®

7.6.8 condition
if + sub-clause

7.6.9 focusing
about (as in: I 'don't ·want to ˏtalk about the ·war.**), on (as in:** I 'cannot ·give you ·any information on ·train ·services.**) ®,**
only (as in: I 'only ·wanted to ˅help.**)**

8 Deixis

Deixis involves referring or identifying by means of linguistic items belonging to closed sets the reference of which is dependent upon the context of the utterance (e.g. time, place, persons involved). Deixis may be definite or indefinite (*he* vs. *someone*), non-anaphoric or anaphoric (i.e. referring to an item already mentioned) ('Why don't you ˏcome? vs. I'll ˋbuy those ˏbooks | because I ˏneed them.)

8.1. *definite*

8.1.1 non-anaphoric
personal pronouns (subject forms and object forms)
possessive adjectives: **my, your,** etc.
possessive pronouns as complement (as in: 'This is ˏmine.)
possessive pronouns as subject **®** (as in: 'Mine is ˏbetter.)
demonstrative adjectives and pronouns: **this, that, these, those, such**
independent relative pronoun:
what (as in: 'What you ·say is ˏtrue.)
definite article: **the**
interrogative pronouns: **who, whom ®, whose ®, what, which**
interrogative adjectives: **whose ®, what, which**

8.1.2 anaphoric
personal pronouns (subject forms and object forms)
possessive adjectives
possessive pronouns as complement (as in: ˋYou ·take it, it's ˋyours.)
demonstrative adjectives and pronouns
relative pronouns: **who, whom ® whose ®, which, that ®,** omission of relative pronoun **®**
reflexive/emphatic pronouns: **my·self, yourself,** etc. (as in: I ˏhurt myself; I've 'done it my ˏself.)
reciprocal pronoun: **each other**
definite article: **the**
adverbs: **here, there, now, then, so** (as in: He ˅wanted to ·go ·out | but he 'didn't ˏsay so.)
prop word: **one, ones** (as in: I 'like the ˋred one.)
substitute-verb: **do** (as in: He ˅asked me to ·help him, | and I ˏdid.)

8.2 *indefinite*
indefinite article: **a, an**
indefinite pronouns: **someone, somebody, no one, (not) ... anybody, (not) ... anyone, nobody, each, everybody, everyone, something, (not) ... anything, nothing, everything, all** (as in: They 'all went ˏhome; I ·want ˋall of it.),
both (as in: They 'both went ˏhome; I ·want ˏboth of them.),

some (as in: 'Some of them ·went ˌhome.), it (as in: It's ˌraining.), you (as in: It's a 'nice ˌrecord | if you ˇlike ·modern ·music.)

indefinite determiners:
See General Notions 4.2.
adverbs: somewhere, nowhere, everywhere, (not) ... anywhere, sometimes, never, always
semi-deictics: person (as in: There are 'five ·persons ˌpresent.) Ⓡ, **man** Ⓡ (as in: There were ˇanimals ·here | be'fore ˌman ·came.) **people (as in:** 'What do ·people ·think about the ˌgovernment?; There are 'five ·people ˌpresent.), **thing (as in:** 'What do you ˌcall that ·thing?), **do (as in:** 'What are you ·going to ·do toˌnight?)

7 Specific notions

Introduction

In the following list the *specific notions* for *Threshold Level* are arranged under 14 themes:

1 personal identification

2 house and home, environment

3 daily life

4 free time, entertainment

5 travel

6 relations with other people

7 health and body care

8 education

9 shopping

10 food and drink

11 services

12 places

13 language

14 weather

The themes may relate to the situational context in which particular transactions may take place (e.g. buying something in a shop) as well as to topics for communicative interaction (e.g. talking about shopping facilities). Under the title of each theme an indication is given as to what learners at *Threshold Level* may be expected to be able to do with regard to it. These indications are necessarily incomplete and are to be supplemented from other components of our specification.

To facilitate reference, the *specific notions* are further arranged under sub-themes. In the same way as the *general notions*, the *specific notions* are indicated by means of their (recommended) exponents (see the introduction to the list of *general notions*). Alternative exponents of essentially the same notion are presented thus: first name/Christian name/forename/given name. In such a case the learner should be able to use at least one of them productively but to understand all the others.

The specification contains several open-ended items indicated by italics (e.g. *names of occupations*). In these cases we leave it to materials designers, teachers and learners to identify those specific notions, if any, which suit their own purposes. In order to provide some guidance as to those notions, which, in our view, might be primarily considered we add, in a number of cases, a list of them preceded by 'e.g.' It should be understood, however, that the notions in such lists are merely offered by way of suggestion and have not got the status of definitely recommended ones. If a word may be used in different meanings, the meaning intended usually follows from its inclusion under a particular sub-theme (e.g. **tip** under 'eating and drinking out') or it is clarified by means of contextualisation (e.g. **letter:** What's the last letter of your name?). These illustrative sentences have no other role than clarification of the meaning of the word involved; they are not meant as recommended phrases for inclusion in course materials.

Specific notions for *Threshold Level* including recommended exponents

....

1   Personal identification

The learners can say who they are, spell their name, state their address, give their telephone number, say when and where they were born, state their age, sex, say whether they are married or not, state their nationality, say where they are from, what they do for a living, describe their family, state their religion, if any, state their likes and dislikes, say what other people are like; elicit/understand similar information from others.

1.1   **name**

name

first name/Christian name/forename

surname/family name

initials ®

Mr ...

Mrs ...

Miss ...

Ms ... (writing)

to write/to spell
'How do you ·write/spell your ˌname?

names of letters of the alphabet

to call
We ·call him ˌBill.

to be/to be called
He's (·called) ˌBill.

to sign ®

signature ®

letter
'What's the ·last ·letter of your ˌname?

1.2   **address**

to live
'Where do you ˌlive?

address
'What's your adˌdress?

names of roads etc. e.g. park, road, square, street

number
I ·live at 'number fifˌteen.

country
I ·live in the ˌcountry.

town/city

village

names of countries e.g. Britain, Germany, Russia, Spain, Switzerland, the United States

names of cities e.g. Athens, Basle, Brussels, Cologne, Copenhagen, Florence, Lisbon, The Hague, Vienna

1.3 telephone number
(See also Specific Notions 11.2.)

telephone
'Have you ·got a ‚telephone?

to call/to phone/to ring up

telephone number

0 (pronounced [əʊ] in telephone numbers)

1.4 date and place of birth

to be born
I was 'born in ‚London on ...

date

place

birthday

names of the months

the required numerals

1.5 age
See General Notions 5.1.10.

1.6 sex

sex ®

man

woman

boy

girl

male ®

female ®

gentleman (as on lavatory doors) ®

ladies (as on lavatory doors) ®

1.7 marital status

(not/un-)married

single ®

divorced

separated ®

widowed ®

widow

widower

1.8 nationality

nationality ®

names of nationalities e.g. American, Cypriot, Dutch, French, German, Swiss

foreign

foreigner

1.9 origin

to be from ...
I'm from ‚London.
'Where are you ‚from?

to come from ... ®

1.10 occupation

job/occupation/profession

to do

What do you do (for a living)?

names of occupations

e.g. baker, businessman, businesswoman, butcher, civil servant, doctor/physician, greengrocer, grocer, labourer, nurse, clerk, salesman, saleswoman, secretary, shop-assistant, soldier, teacher, tradesman, typist; farm worker, office worker

names of places of work

e.g. factory, farm, hospital, office, school, shop

names of occupational activities

e.g. to buy, to teach, to sell, to work **(as in:** I ·work in an ʼoffice.**)**

worker/employee

boss/employer

manager

firm/company

to work
ʼWhere do you ˌwork?

1.11   family

family
ʼHave you ʼbrought your ˌfamily?
ʼHave you any ˌfamily?

parents/father and mother

child

baby

husband

wife

names of relatives
e.g. aunt, brother, cousin, daughter, father, grandchild, grandfather, grandmother, mother, sister, uncle

1.12   religion

religion ®

names of religions e.g. Christianity (Christian, Orthodox, Catholic, Protestant), Islam (Muslim), Judaism (Jew), atheism (atheist)

god

God

to believe in ...

church

cathedral ®

temple ®

mosque ®

service ®

There are ʼthree ˌservices on ·Sundays.

1.13   likes and dislikes
See Language Functions 2.32–34, objects of likes and dislikes to be derived from other themes.

1.14   character, disposition

What sort of ...?
ʼWhat ·sort of ·man/·woman/ etc./ˌis he/she?

kind
He is a ʼvery ·kind ˌperson.

nice

good

bad

(un)pleasant

quiet ®

active ®

lazy ®

(un-)intelligent

(un-)generous ®

1.15   physical appearance

tall

short

fat

thin

slim

pretty

beautiful

plain

ugly

dark (-haired)

fair (-haired)

bald

2 House and home, environment

The learners can describe a house or flat and the rooms in it, refer to furniture and bedclothes, cost, services and amenities, describe regions and natural environment; obtain/understand similar descriptions and references from others; exchange views on these matters.

2.1 types of accommodation

house

flat

apartment ®

building
I 'have a ‚flat | in a 'big ‚building.

(un-)furnished

to buy

to rent

2.2 accommodation, rooms

room
We have 'two ‚rooms | on the 'ground ‚floor.
We have 'plenty of ‚room ·here.

names of rooms
e.g. bathroom, bedroom, cellar, kitchen, lavatory/toilet/w.c., living-room

floor
The ᵛbedrooms | are on the 'first ‚floor.

basement ®

stairs

downstairs
The 'kitchen is ·down‚stairs.
'Let's go down‚stairs.

upstairs
The 'bathroom is up‚stairs.
'Let's go up‚stairs.

lift

window

door

wall

cupboard ®

garden

2.3 furniture, bedclothes

furniture

names of pieces of furniture
e.g. bed, chair, curtain, desk, lamp, table

blanket

pillow

sheet

quilt

2.4 cost
(See also General Notions 5.2.1.)

price

to be
The ·room is '£55 per ‚week.

rent

to let
'Rooms to ·let.

for sale
'House for ·sale.

included ®
'Water is included in the ‚rent.

2.5 services

electricity

gas

heating

central heating

telephone

water

on
The 'heating is ‚on.

off
The 'heating is ‚off.

to turn on
'Turn on the ‚light ·please.

to turn off
'How do you ·turn off the
ˌheating?

2.6   **amenities**

bath

shower

fridge

television

radio

garage

washing-machine

to clean
The ·rooms are ·cleaned 'twice a
ˌweek.

to wash
You can 'wash your ·clothes
downˌstairs.

2.7   **region**

part of the country
In ᵛour ·part of the ·country |
there are many ˌfactories.

area ®

farmland ®

industry ®

farm

factory

fields

forest/wood

hill

lake

valley

mountain

canal

river

sea

seaside ®

coast ®

beach

island

water

land

top
We could ·see the 'tops of the
ˌmountains.

bottom
We could ·see the 'bottom of the
ˌlake.

flat
ᵛOur ·part of the ·country | is
'quite ˌflat.

2.8   **flora and fauna**

animal

pet

names of animals, birds, fish,
insects
e.g. bird, cat, cow, dog, fish, fly,
goat, horse, insect, pig, sheep

plant

tree

flower

bush

names of plants, trees, flowers
e.g. daffodil, fuchsia, grass, oak,
pine

3 Daily life

The learners can describe their daily routines, at home and at work, can give information about income, schooling and prospects; obtain/understand similar information from others; exchange views on these matters.

3.1 at home
(See also Specific Notions, Section 4.)

to wake up

to get up

to wash

to take a bath

to take a shower

to get (un-)dressed

to have breakfast, etc.

names of meals
e.g. breakfast, lunch, tea, dinner, supper

to cook
I'll 'cook din‚ner for you.

to make
'Shall I ·make a ·pot of ‚tea?

to wash up

to clean
I ·clean the ·windows 'once a ‚week.

to go shopping

to go to school

to go to work

to come home

to go to bed

to go to sleep

spare time

3.2 at work
(See also Specific Notions 1.10.)

working hours

to start work

to stop work

break

holiday(s)

canteen

free
We get a 'free ‚meal | 'every ‚day.

to be free
We are ‛free | on ‚Saturdays.

days off
We have 'two ·days ·off a ‚week.

colleague

(on) strike

unemployment

social security/social benefits

3.3 income

income/salary/wages

to earn

tax(es)

pension

grant ®

allowance ®

3.4 schooling
See Specific Notions, Section 8.

3.5 prospects

to become
I 'may become a ‚doctor.

to learn

to study

to qualify as

to apply (for)
I 'won't apply for ᵛthat ·job.

4   Free time, entertainment

The learners can say when they are free and what they do in their spare time, particularly with reference to hobbies and interests, public entertainment and private pursuits, mass media, sports and reading; obtain/understand similar information from others; exchange views on these matters; make use of entertainment facilities.

4.1   leisure

to be free
I'm 'free ·after ˌsix.

free time/spare time/leisure

holiday(s)

to go out

4.1   hobbies and interests
(See also Language Functions 2.32–34.)

hobby

names of hobbies
e.g. carpentry, collecting stamps, fishing, gardening, knitting, photography, sailing

names of fields of interest
e.g. computers, films, music, politics, sports

to go for ...
I 'always ·go for a ˌwalk | on ˌSundays.

4.3   radio, TV, etc.

radio

to listen to (the radio)

television/TV

to watch (TV)

cable television ®

network

programme

names of radio/TV programmes
e.g. current affairs, comedy, documentary, drama, film, news, quiz, commercials

cassette recorder

tape recorder ®

tape

cassette

walkman ®

video recorder

videotape

record/gramophone record

record player

CD/compact disc

CD player

to play
'Let's ·play your ·new ˌrecord.

song

names of types of music
e.g. classical, folk, jazz, modern music, pop music

to show
'What are they ·showing on TˌV to·night?

4.4   cinema, theatre

names of places for public entertainment concert, etc.
e.g. cabaret, cinema, circus, disco, night-club, theatre

names of public performances
e.g. ballet, concert, film, floor show, musical, opera, revue, show

names of types of performers
e.g. actor, actress, ballet dancer, disc jockey, (film) star, musician, pop star, singer

names of musical instruments
e.g. flute, piano, violin, guitar

to dance

to play
'Who is ·playing ˏHamlet?
She ·plays the guiˏtar.

to sing

performance ®

ticket
'I'll ·get the ˏtickets.

ticket office ®

booking office ®

afternoon performance ®

matinee ®

seat

row ®
We ·have ·seats in 'row ˏfive.

front
We have ·seats in the ˏfront.

centre

back
'Two ·seats at the ˏback, ·please.

entrance ®

exit ®

emergency exit ®

cloakroom ®

lavatory/toilet/w.c.

programme
'Shall I ·buy a ˏprogramme?

interval ®

4.5 exhibitions, museums, etc.

museum

gallery ®

art gallery ®

exhibition ®

art

picture/painting

sculpture ®

modern

old

antique ®

open
'Open on ˏSundays | 2–5 p.ˏm.

opening-hours ®

closed

to close
The mu·seum 'closes at ˏsix.

closing time

4.6 intellectual and artistic pursuits

to read

to study

to learn

book

story

poem

names of types of books
e.g. biography, detective story, novel, short story, spy story, thriller

bookshop

library

to write

to make
He 'made a ·picture of a ˏbridge.

names of art forms
e.g. painting, photography, sculpture

4.7 sports

sport(s)

names of sports and games
e.g. baseball, chess, cricket, football, hockey, (horse) racing, riding, snooker, (lawn) tennis, rugby, skiing, swimming

to play
I've 'never ˋplayed ˏhockey.

(playing·) cards

to watch

race

to race

game

to win

to lose

draw
The 'game ·ended in a ‚draw.

player

team

club

field

ground
We 'live near the ‚football ·ground.

stadium

ball

against
We 'saw ·England against ‚France | in '6‚8.

4.8 **press**

newspaper/paper

magazine
'Let's ·buy some maga‚zines.

article

picture

advertisement

page

reporter/journalist

to read

· ·

5   Travel

The learners can use and refer to means of transport; travel by road, rail, sea and air for business and holiday purposes.

5.1 **public transport**

to go
'How can I ·go to ‚Liverpool?

to travel

traveller ®

passenger ®

to travel by air, train, bus, etc.

journey

aeroplane ®

plane

airport

airline

terminal
Your ·flight is from 'terminal ‚A.

to check in

boarding-pass ®

flight ®
·Flight 'KL 17‚5 | has 'just ar‚rived. En'joy your ‚flight.

charter flight ®

to fly

security (as in: security check) ®

gate ®
The 'flight to ·New ‚York | is from 'gate ‚10.

to board

stewardess/hostess

bus

coach

bus stop

driver

train

underground
'Let's ·take the ‚underground.

(railway) station

railways ®

platform
Our ·train ·leaves from 'platform ‚10.

to change
For ˅Leeds | you ·have to ·change at ˋSheffield.

connection ®
We'll 'miss our con'nection | to 'Reading!

fast train

slow train

tram

tram stop

boat

ferry ®

ship ®

quay

cabin

harbour ®

taxi/cab

taxi rank/cab rank

taxi driver, cab driver ®

booking-office

to book

time table

fare ®
'What's the ·fare to ˌLiverpool?

ticket

adult
'One ˌadult | and 'two ˌchildren.

single
'Two ·singles to ˌBrighton, ·please.

return
A re'turn ·ticket is 'cheaper | than ·two ˌsingles.

class
I 'always ·travel ˌsecond ·class.

business class ®

tourist class ®

to smoke

waiting-room

lounge

arrival ®

departure ®

luggage/baggage

lost property office ®

travel bureau ®

information office ®

information desk ®

enquiries ®

restaurant

refreshments ®

bar

delay ®

to be delayed ®

to cancel
'Has our ·flight been ˌcancelled?

5.2 **private transport** (See also Specific Notions 5.3, 11.8 and 11.9.)
names of vehicles
e.g. bike/bicycle, car, lorry, motor cycle, scooter, van

to drive

driver

to ride

cyclist

to hire/to rent
We could 'always ·rent a ᵛcar.

5.3 **traffic**

street ®

one-way street ®

road

main road

motorway

bridge

crossing

level crossing ®

roundabout ®

to cross
'Don't ·cross ᵛhere!

corner

traffic lights

blue zone ®
In the 'blue ‚zone | you can ·park for 'one ·hour ‚only.

speed

speed limit

fine ®
You'll ·have to ·pay a ·fine of '£‚10.

danger ®

dangerous

safe

safety ®

safety belt ®

signpost

to follow
'Follow the ‚signs.

pedestrian ®

map

distance ®

to lose one's way

common road-sign texts (reading only)
e.g. cross now, exit, give way, keep left, keep right, no parking, no waiting, one way, stop, turn left, turn right

5.4　**holidays**

journey

trip

tour

guided tour ®

tourist

tourist office

(tourist) guide

group
We 'went with a ·group of ‚tourists.

to visit

sights ®

names of sights and buildings of interest
e.g. castle, cathedral, ruins, zoo

abroad ®
'Are you ·going a‚broad ·this ·year?

to a foreign country
'Are you ·going to a ·foreign ‚country ·this ·year?

names of continents: Africa, America, Asia, Australia, Europe

5.5　**accommodation**

names of types of accommodation for travellers
e.g. camp site, guest house, hotel, inn, tent, youth hostel

single room

double room

full board ®

half board ®

bed and breakfast

balcony

view ®

guest

to book

reservation ®

reception ®

desk ®
'Please ·leave your ·key at the ‚desk.

to register ®

registration form ®

key

to call
'Can you ·call me at ‚six, ·please?

message
'Is there a ‚message for me?

hall

lounge ®

lift

to press ®

button
'Press the ‚button | for the 'third ‚floor.

to push ®
‚Push | to 'open the ‚door.

to pull ®
‚Pull | to 'open the ‚door.

fire
In 'case of ‚fire | …

to check out ®

bill
'Can I have my ‚bill, ·please?

receipt

cheque

to pay cash

credit card

5.6 **luggage**

luggage/baggage

bag

suitcase

box

camera

porter ®
'Do you ·want a ‚porter for your ·luggage?

locker ®

5.7 **entering and leaving a country**

frontier/border

immigration ®

passport control ®

visa ®

customs

to import ®

to declare ®
'Have you ·anything to de‚clare?

to open
'Will you ·open your ‚bag, ·please?

duty ®
You'll 'have to ·pay `duty | on ‚this.

duty-free ®

money

to change
I ·want to ·change '500 ‚dollars.

currency ®

5.8 **travel documents**

document ®

passport

insurance

driving licence ®

· ·

6 Relations with other people

The learners can refer to personal relations, participate in social life, deal with matters of correspondence, refer to club membership, refer to forms of government and politics, to matters of crime and justice, of war and peace, to social affairs; exchange information and views on these subjects with others.

6.1 **relationship**

acquaintance

friend

boy-friend

girl-friend

lover

partner

stranger

6.2 **invitations**

to invite

invitation

to make an appointment

to join ®
'Will you ·join us for ˌlunch?

to expect ®
We'll 'expect you at ˌsix.

to visit

to come and see ... ®
'Why don't you ·come and ˌsee us to·night?

party
We're 'having a ˋparty | toˌnight.

to talk

to dance

present
He ·brought a ˋpresent for me.

guest

6.3   **correspondence**

to correspond with ... ®

to write (to)

pen friend ®

letter

envelope

postcard

note paper

paper
'Have you ·got some ˌpaper for me?

stamp

airmail

pen

pencil

ball point/ball pen/biro

to send
I'll 'send you a ˌpostcard.

to receive/to get
I ·got a ˌletter from her.

answer

to answer

6.4   **club membership**

club

member

meeting

to meet
We ·meet 'every ˌWednesday.

6.5   **government and politics**

to govern

government

parliament

president

king

queen

prince

princess

minister

prime minister

to elect ®

election

to vote

politics

political

party
'Are you a ·party ˌmember?

names of political parties
e.g. communist, conservative, liberal, socialist

right wing

left wing

leader
He is the 'leader of the conˌservatives.

state
The ·state ·owns 'many ˌfactories.

EU/European Union

NATO [neɪtəʊ]

6.6   **crime and justice**

crime

criminal
He is a ˌcriminal.

to steal

thief
burglar ®
burglary ®
theft ®
to rob
robber
robbery
to kill
to murder ®
killer/murderer
to kidnap
kidnapper
to hijack
hijacker
to rape
rape
to shoot
gun
bomb
to throw
The 'kidnapper ·threw a ˌbomb |
into the ˌgarage.
terrorist
terrorism
drugs
to take drugs
addict
alcohol
victim
police
policeman
policewoman
police station
to arrest
law
lawyer
judge
jury
court

witness ®
prison
to punish
punishment

6.7 **war and peace**
peace
disarmament
war
to fight
army
navy
air force
soldier
officer
enemy
ally
battle
attack
to attack
defence
to defend
victory ®
defeat ®
(nuclear) weapon ®
gun
bullet
bomb
missile
spy

6.8 **social affairs**
issue ®
pollution
poverty
problem
question
welfare
rich
poor

··

7   Health and body care

The learners can refer to matters of personal comfort, stating whether they feel well, are hungry, tired, etc., refer to matters of personal hygiene and obtain the articles required, refer to matters of health and illness and describe what is wrong to a doctor or dentist, report accidents, refer to medical services and insurance; exchange information and views on these matters.

7.1   parts of the body

names of parts of the body
e.g. arm, back, chest, foot, hair, hand, head, heart, leg, lungs, neck, stomach, tooth

7.2   personal comfort

comfortable
I'm 'quite ˌcomfortable | ˌnow.
The ·chair 'isn't very
ᵛcomfortable.

hunger ℞

hungry

thirst ℞

thirsty

tired

to rest
I'd 'like to ˌrest a ·little.

sleepy

to sleep

to wake up

to feel well

to look well

7.3   hygiene

clean

dirty

brush

comb

razor

sanitary towel ℞

scissors

soap

toothbrush

toothpaste

towel

to cut
'Will you ·cut my ˌhair, ·please?

to shave

to wash
I'd 'like to ˌwash before ·dinner.
'Can you ·wash these ˌclothes for me?

laundry ℞
'Is there a ˌlaundry ·here?
'Has the ·laundry come ˌback ·yet?

7.4   ailments, accidents

health ℞

ill

to fall ill ℞

to feel ill

to be alive/to live

dead

killed ℞

disease ℞

illness ℞

pain/-ache
I have a ˌheadache.

fever/temperature

to have a cold

dizzy

to feel sick

to hurt

names of diseases **e.g.** AIDS ℞, diabetes, diarrhoea, influenza (flu), V.D. ℞

operation
I 'had an ope‚ration | ·last ‚year.

to be operated upon ®

accident

to fall

to break
He has 'broken his ‚leg.

to burn
He has 'burnt his ‚hand.

to cut
She has 'cut her ‚finger.

wound

bandage/dressing

diet ®

7.5 medical services

dentist

doctor

nurse

specialist

chemist

medicine
'Do you ·take any ‚medicine?

tablet
·Take 'three ·tablets a ‚day.

pill ®

ambulance

hospital

ward ®
The 'patient is in the ‚children's
·ward.

patient ®
The ·patient is 'waiting.

to fill ®
This ·tooth was ·filled 'six
‚months a·go.

appointment ®
'What ·time is your
ap‚pointment?

to see a doctor (dentist, etc.)

prescription ®

glasses

7.6 insurance

to insure

insurance

third-party
'Do you have ·third-·party
‚insurance?

....

8 Education

The learners can exchange information and views on educational
matters, particularly types of education, school subjects and
qualifications.

8.1 schooling

education

to learn

to take a course, lessons, etc.

to teach

to train
He (was) 'trained to be a ‚nurse.

lesson

course
I 'took a ·course in mathe‚matics.

lecture ®

teacher

master ®

professor

student

pupil

names of types of education
e.g. primary school, secondary
school, university, college, adult
education

8.2   subjects

subject
'What ˌsubjects did you ·take at
·school?

names of school subjects
e.g. arithmetic, computer
science, economics, geography,
history, mathematics, physics,
reading, science, writing

8.3   qualifications

diploma

certificate ®

examination

final examination ®

entrance examination ®

test

to pass
I 'passed my examˌination | 'last
ˌyear.

to fail
I 'failed my ·driving-·test ˌtwice.

· ·

9   Shopping

The learners can use shopping facilities, particularly obtaining
foodstuffs, clothes, household articles and smokers' requisites, discuss
prices, pay for things bought; exchange information and views on
these matters. For each of the following sub-themes, see also under
General Notions, particularly 2.8.1, 5.1.1, 5.1.8–9, 5.1.14, 5.2.1–2.

9.1   shopping facilities

shop

to go shopping

supermarket

department store ®

market

self-service

names of types of shops
e.g. baker's, butcher's,
greengrocer's, grocer's,
tobacconist's

sale
I've 'bought ˋthis | at the ˌsales.

it is my (etc.) turn ®

to show

to wrap up ®

to change
I 'want to ·change this ˌshirt; | it
is 'not the ·right ˌcolour.

9.2   foodstuffs
See Specific Notions 10.1.

9.3   clothes, fashion
(See also General Notions
2.8.1 and 5.1.9.)

clothes

names of clothes
e.g. blouse, coat, dress, hat,
jacket, raincoats, shirt, shoes,
skirt, socks, stockings, suit,
tights, trousers, underwear

pocket

purse

wallet

handbag

jewellery ®

watch
'Have you ·got a ·new ˌwatch?

to try on

to put on (clothes)

to take off (clothes)

to wear (clothes)

9.4   smoking

tobacco

pipe
cigar
cigarette
ashtray
to smoke
no smoking

9.5 **household articles**
fork
knife
spoon
dish
plate
Be ᵛcareful, | the ·plate is ᵛhot.
cup
saucer
bottle
pot
glass

jar
jug
matches
string

9.6 **prices**
(See also General Notions
5.2.1.)
to pay
to spend
money
discount ®
bank-notes
coins
credit card
£ (pound)
p (penny)
names of national currencies
e.g. cent, dollar, franc, mark

10 Food and drink

The learners can refer to and order various kinds of food and beverage, also in a restaurant, café, etc.; exchange information and views on food, drink and places for eating and drinking.

10.1 **types of food and drink**
(See also General Notions
5.1.6.)
to eat
meal
snack
names of meals
e.g. breakfast, lunch, tea, dinner, supper
to have breakfast, etc.
course
'What's the ˌmain ·course?
vegetables
names of vegetables
e.g. beans, cabbage, carrots, cauliflower, mushrooms, peas, potatoes, spinach

chips
salad
soup
meat
names of kinds of meat
e.g. beef, lamb, mutton, pork, veal
names of meat products
e.g. hamburger, sausage(s)
fish
names of kinds of fish
e.g. cod, plaice, sole
poultry ®
names of kinds of poultry
e.g. chicken, turkey
egg

omelette

cheese

dessert

sweet ®
'Would you ·like a ,sweet?

ice-cream

vanilla

chocolate
'Would you ·like a ·piece of
,chocolate?
'Chocolate ·ice-,cream, ·please.

cake

pastry

pie

tart

fruit

names of fruits
e.g. apple, banana, grape,
lemon, nut, orange, raisin, pear,
strawberry

mustard

pepper

salt

oil

vinegar

flour

bread

piece
'Would you ·like a ·piece of
,cake?

slice

(bread) roll

sandwich

toast

butter

peanut butter

jam

to drink

coffee

tea

cream

milk

sugar

drink
'Would you ·like a ,drink?

names of beverages
e.g. beer, fruit juice, mineral
water, soft drinks, orange juice,
water, wine

ways of preparing food
e.g. to bake, to boil, to fry, to
grill, to mix, to peel, to stir

fresh, freshly

10.2   eating and drinking out

snack bar

coffee shop

café

pub

bar

canteen

self-service

help-yourself ®

to serve

service ®
'No ·service in the ,garden.
'Service is in·cluded in the ,bill.

waiter

waitress

menu

to choose

to decide ®
'Have you de,cided ·yet?

to order

bill

tip ®

service charge ®

to take away ®
'Can I ·take this a,way?

11 Services

The learners can refer to, enquire about and make use of postal services, telephone, telegraph, bank, police, diplomatic services, medical services, car maintenance services and petrol stations.

11.1 post
(See also Specific Notions 6.3.)
post office
to post
postman ®
mail ®
parcel
postage ®
letter box
collection ®
poste-restante ®

11.2 telephone
(See also Specific Notions 1.3.)
telephone booth ®
phone booth ®
call box ®
operator ®
to dial ®
out of order ®

11.3 telegraph
telegraph ®
telegram
word
sender ®
fax

11.4 bank
(See also Specific Notions 9.6.)
bank
to change
I'd 'like to ·change '500 ˌfrancs.
currency ®
cheque
travellers' cheque ®

to cash
I'd 'like to ·cash this ˌcheque.
account
I 'have an ·acˌcount | with the 'Midland ˌBank.
to borrow
to lend

11.5 police
See Specific Notions 6.6.
to lose
I've 'lost my ˌpassport.

11.6 diplomatic services
consul
consulate
embassy
ambassador ®

11.7 hospital, surgery, etc.
See Specific Notions 7.5.

11.8 garage
garage
trouble
engine trouble
brake
engine
lights
steering
to help
to repair
to work
My 'brakes ·don't ·work.

11.9 petrol station
(See also General Notions 2.8.5.)
petrol station

petrol	tyres
unleaded	to check
oil	empty
oil change ®	full

12   Places

The learners can ask the way and give strangers directions. See General Notions 2.1–2.5 and Specific Notions 1.2 and 5.3.

13   Language

The learners can refer to foreign-language ability and deal with problems of understanding and expression.

13.1   **ability, understanding, expression**

See Language Functions 6.1–6.10 and General Notions 5.2.7 and 5.2.13. In addition:

language
to read
to speak
to pronounce
to understand
to write
well
I 'cannot ˌwrite ·English ·very ·well.
a little

not at all
to translate
translation
to interpret
dictionary
question
'May I ·ask a ˌquestion?
clear
It's 'not ˌclear to me.
to explain
mistake
names of languages
e.g. French, German, English, Spanish, Italian, Dutch, Swedish, Russian

14   Weather

The learners can understand a weather forecast and exchange information and views on climate and weather conditions.

14.1   **climate and weather**

climate
weather
sun
sunny

sunshine
to shine
rain
rainy
to rain

fog
foggy
mist ®
snow
to snow
ice
frost
to freeze
wind
storm

gale
thunderstorm
snowstorm
lightning
fine ®
It will be ˋfine | to‚morrow.
mild
shade
ˈShall we ·sit in the ‚shade?

8 Verbal exchange patterns

Exponents of single language functions may occur in isolation. 'Stop!' as an order, and 'Look out!' as a warning, are obvious examples. On the whole, however, function exponents are more likely to occur in sequences. Such sequences will usually exhibit certain regularities in the order of their elements. Thus, an apology will very often be followed by an explanation: 'I'm sorry I'm late, but I had to see my dentist first.' Such more or less regularly occurring combinations may be referred to as *patterns*. Monologues may be thus patterned, if only in that they may start with an utterance calling for attention and end with one signalling termination. With regard to oral communication involving contributions by the learner the emphasis, at *Threshold Level*, is not so much on monologues as on verbal exchanges between two, or more than two, speakers. In such exchanges the participants may mesh their contributions in accordance with certain conventions. We then speak of verbal exchange patterns. It is a characteristic of these patterns that they are variable, in that a conversation may move in various directions. Especially when they are very short, however, involving only two or three utterances, they may also be standardised. This may be said, for instance, of the typical greeting + response pattern occurring when two people pass each other in the street. The large majority of the verbal exchange patterns, however, that are relevant to *Threshold Level* learners in the light of the objective are variable. We may illustrate this by reproducing two examples of 'predictable fish-and-chip' discourses provided by A. J. Peck in an article called 'Some ideas on teaching discourse synthesis' (the function labels are ours):

1	Sales person	: 'Yes?	asking for wish (opening)
	Customer	: 'Haddock and ˌchips.	expressing wish
	Sales person	: ·That'll be '£1.ˌ20	asking for payment
	Customer	: (Gives money).	(making payment)
	Sales person	: ˌThanks.	thanking (termination)

2	Sales person	: 'Yes?	asking for wish (opening)
	Customer	: 'Fish and ˌchips | – ˌtwice.	expressing wish
	Sales person	: 'Cod, | or ˌplaice?	asking for preference
	Customer	: ˌPlaice.	expressing preference
	Sales person	: 'Large, | or ˌsmall	asking for preference
	Customer	: ˌLarge.	expressing preference
		And 'salt and ˌvinegar.	expressing further wish

Sales person	: ·That'll be '£2.,30	asking for payment
Customer	: (Gives money)	(making payment: non-verbal termination)

Apart from the variability (by no means exhausted here) of the 'fish-and-chips buying dialogue', we note the occurrence of sub-patterns as well as the integration of non-verbal turns. Communicative ability at *Threshold Level* implies the ability to play a part in verbal exchange patterns such as the ones illustrated above.

A number of dialogue types (which may, in fact, involve more than two participants) are explicitly or implicitly covered by our objective. They involve the occurrence of verbal exchange patterns with a certain measure of predictability. They are particularly associated with the following communicative events.

1 making purchases

    a) in a shop

    b) at a ticket counter, ticket from bus conductor, etc.

2 ordering food and drink
    restaurant, canteen, snack bar, etc.

3 making enquiries

    a) non-personal (where to go, where to eat, about opening hours, about various facilities and services, etc.)

    b) personal (about name, address, place of origin, etc.)

4 meeting people

    a) strangers

    b) friends, acquaintances

5 asking and showing the way

6 asking and telling the time

7 inviting and reacting to invitation

8 arranging accommodation

9 proposing a course of action and reacting to such proposals

10 having a discussion
    agreeing/disagreeing, exchanging views, etc.

However predictable the occurrence of certain verbal exchange patterns in the above dialogue types may be, there is always a strong element of unpredictability as well. When the more or less standardised patterns are broken, or even set aside completely, conversation does not lend itself to a didactically meaningful description of the kind we try to provide in this document. 'All we can be said to understand about such talk' Peck observes, 'is that certain elements occur frequently. These act as signposts along a road we are travelling.' He adds: 'We can teach pupils to recognise these elements of discourse and to use them themselves.'

Chapter 5 contains a classified list of the language functions, together with their common exponents, which are combined in verbal interaction. We have not thought it necessary, or even desirable, to attempt to specify the verbal interaction patterns to be used by learners (e.g. in the form of praxeograms).

As we have shown, not even the most routine transactions of daily life are fully predictable. Many conditions may have to be fulfilled before a transaction can be successfully completed. A complex transaction may have to pass through numerous stages of negotiation each involving lengthy verbal exchanges. In routine cases many may be passed over in silence and the exchange limited to a few words on either side. Making travel arrangements, say, may take either form. We all know what it is like to queue behind someone who wishes to travel to a remote place involving different means of transport, choices of route, co-ordination of timetable, comparison of prices using different combinations of various categories of tickets, involving different currencies, wishing to use a foreign credit card, etc., when all one wishes to do oneself is to buy a single ticket to the next station, and the train is due to leave in five minutes. One wishes there were simply a ticket vending machine, in which case no oral interaction need – or indeed can – take place, but instead a set of written instructions must be followed. The example could be paralleled in the settings of shopping, eating out, garages, and others where goods and services are required. In each case the services and/or goods must be identified, made available and paid for. Each stage may be carried out through personal interaction involving more or less verbal interaction or by self-service with or without mechanisation, normally eliminating verbal interaction in favour of written instructions. What is to be done at each stage may be self-evident, requiring no language, or a perfunctory exchange, or a brief unrelated interactional exchange to establish human contact. On the other hand, there may be choices to be exercised, preferences to be expressed, pros and cons to be discussed, conflicts of interest to be resolved, before the decisions can be made on which the next stage depends. At any time, communication difficulties may arise, needing to be dealt with by repair procedures. As social beings we have the larger schemata in our social competence, though it is only in exceptional circumstances that we need to follow the full process through in detail by means of language. In any case:

- the schemata are largely shared by European societies. Where transactions and interactions are governed by different rules, effective communication and co-operation depend, of course, on mutual understanding between participants from different backgrounds (e.g. whether and how bargaining is conducted over prices, whether tipping is expected for small services, etc.);

- the order in which the steps occur is not fixed;

- whether steps are made explicit or passed over in silence depends on the situation and on cultural conventions;

- the ways in which objects are identified, preferences expressed, dissatisfaction or agreement shown and so on are not specific to particular situations (beyond the topic-specific words and expressions required). They are generalisable as resources which can be called on according to need in a wide range of situations. It is this principle which underlies the notional/functional approach as distinct from some other situational approaches.

For these reasons, we do not specify here in an exhaustive way the patterns of verbal interaction which a learner should be able to carry through in the situations envisaged. To attempt to do so would be at once too restrictive and over elaborate. In some cases (e.g. *having a discussion*) the possibilities of combining speech acts are virtually unlimited. In others (e.g. *asking and telling the time*) a two-term exchange normally suffices, apart from non-specific opening and closing exchanges. A general schema, such as that presented below, may however be set up to cover, with certain adaptations, the various transactions involving the purchase of goods and services.

General schema for purchase of goods or services

1 Moving to place of transaction

  1.1 Finding the way to the shop, store, supermarket, restaurant, station, hotel, etc.

  1.2 Finding the way to the counter, department, table, ticket office, reception, etc.

2 Establishing contact

  2.1 Exchanging greetings with the shopkeeper/assistant/waiter/receptionist, etc.

    2.1.1 assistant greets

    2.1.2 customer greets

3 Selecting goods/services

   3.1 identifying category of goods/services required

      3.1.1 seeking information

      3.1.2 giving information

   3.2 identifying options

   3.3 discussing pros and cons of options (e.g. quality, price, colour, size of goods)

      3.3.1 seeking information

      3.3.2 giving information

      3.3.3 seeking advice

      3.3.4 giving advice

      3.3.5 asking for preference

      3.3.6 expressing preference etc.

   3.4 identifying particular goods required

   3.5 examining goods

   3.6 agreeing to purchase

4 Exchanging goods for payment

   4.1 agreeing prices of items

   4.2 agreeing addition of total

   4.3 receiving/handing over payment

   4.4 receiving/handing over goods (and receipt)

   4.5 exchanging thanks

      4.5.1 assistant thanks

      4.5.2 customer thanks

5 Leave taking

   5.1 expressing (mutual) satisfaction

      5.1.1 assistant expresses satisfaction

      5.1.2 customer expresses satisfaction

   5.2 exchanging interpersonal comment (e.g. weather, local gossip)

   5.3 exchanging parting greetings

      5.3.1 assistant greets

      5.3.2 customer greets

It will be seen that the sequence is not strictly linear. In hotels and restaurants 4.5 may come between 3.4 and 3.5, payment being made normally at the end of the meal or period of residence. In a village shop elements of 5.2 may be interspersed with any of the other stages. In the case of supermarkets and especially mechanised vending machines 2 and 5 do not apply. 3.1–3.6 and 4.5–4.6 are carried out in silence by the customer in 'dialogue' with written descriptions and instructions – a process often preferred by foreign visitors and even native speakers as avoidance strategies against expected difficulties of interpersonal communication.

It will also be seen that (4) is central. A minimal interaction consists of 4.4 and 4.5, performed by actions without words.

Peck 1: 3.1.1–3.4–4.1–(4.3)–4.5.1

Peck 2: 3.1.1–3.1.2–3.2–3.4–3.2–3.4–3.4–4.1–(4.3)–(4.4)

Peck's examples are brief and businesslike, in a situation where choice is extremely restricted and prices are fixed. Other situations (e.g. a celebratory meal in an expensive restaurant, buying an expensive dress in a prestigious store) would call on more of the resources implied, as might the selection of hotel accommodation or the kind of complex travel arrangements outlined earlier.

9 Dealing with texts: reading and listening

In item 3 of the *extended characterisation* the ability to deal with written and spoken texts that is expected of learners at *Threshold Level* is related – and confined – to texts relevant to certain specified situations and to certain specified topics. What the learners can do with regard to these texts – the 'tasks' they can perform – is described in the same item as 'understanding the gist and/or relevant details'. In carrying out these tasks the learners may have to use certain interpretation strategies as listed under item 5 of the *extended characterisation*:

- distinguishing main points and secondary points

- distinguishing fact from comment

- identifying relevant information

- making use of clues such as titles, illustrations, typography (e.g. bolding, italics, capitals), paragraphing, and, in oral texts, discourse markers such as phrasing, the placing of emphasis, structurally relevant pauses, tone of voice, etc.

The nature of the texts to be understood is further defined by the following criteria:

- they have a clear structure, both conceptually and formally

- the information contained in them is exclusively or mainly offered explicitly

- their understanding presupposes little or no familiarity with specific features of a foreign culture, other than 'general European culture'

- they are produced in an easily accessible form.

No limitation is put on the kind of information to be understood from a text as defined above. This means that the understanding is not confined to factual information but may equally concern the expression of opinions, attitudes, moods and wishes, provided that particularly the second criterion above is satisfied.

No indications are given as to the range and nature of the lexical content of texts to be understood. When a learner can use the strategies listed as I.1–5 and II.1–4 in the chapter on 'compensation strategies' (Chapter 12), there is no point in trying to specify the limits of the vocabulary content that the learners may be supposed to be able to deal with. This is all the more valid for reading, if the learners have access to a dictionary and know how to use it. It is assumed that with these devices and the command of a core vocabulary such as the one recommended in this volume the learners' range of action – particularly as readers – is, as far as vocabulary is concerned, sufficient for the kinds of texts that fall within the terms of our definition. Only one further, and obvious, reservation has to be made with regard to vocabulary, and that is that the learners cannot be expected to be able to understand items whose meaning, in the available context, would be obscure to them even if the text had been produced in their native language. This would apply to items whose meaning would be, conceptually, beyond the learners' mental reach. They would be unlikely to occur, however, in texts referred to in this specification.

Although an exhaustive enumeration of text types that the learner at *Threshold Level* will be able to deal with is not possible, we shall list, by way of guidance and exemplification, those text types that at this level would seem to be particularly relevant in connection with the situations and the topics mentioned in items 1 and 2 of the *extended characterisation*. By 'relevant' we mean 'relevant to the learners' needs and interests', and the implication of 'at this level' is that we exclude those text types which would be likely to make a much greater demand on the learners' familiarity with the foreign language than may be expected at *Threshold Level*. The latter restriction leads to the exclusion of, for instance, the text type 'rules and regulations', which often requires familiarity with a highly formal register.

Reading

Text types related to the situations of the *extended characterisation*:

Signs (e.g. street signs), directions (e.g. how to make a phone call), notices, instructions (e.g. warnings), posters, advertisements, brochures, leaflets, guides (e.g. hotel guides, city guides), price lists, timetables, bills, tickets, radio/TV/theatre programmes, legends (of maps), telephone directories, forms (e.g. landing forms, hotel registration forms), shop signs, product packaging (e.g. in supermarkets), instructions on automatic vending machines.

Text types related to the topics of the *extended characterisation*:

In addition to several text types listed under 'situations' above, the following:

personal correspondence (letters, postcards, telegrams); informative articles, features, weather forecasts, *from* newspapers and magazines.

Listening

The range of text types proposed for listening is considerably narrower than that for reading. Generally, the understanding of orally produced texts is subject to time constraints: they are produced only once and in a linear form which does not allow the listener to go back to earlier parts or to reflect on the text as a whole as easily as may be done with written texts. It would, therefore, be unrealistic to expect a listening ability fully corresponding to what was included under 'reading'. Such texts as news programmes on radio and especially on television with its stronger visual support may be partly understood by learners at *Threshold Level* but because of their low degree of predictability we would situate a general ability to understand their gist and/or relevant details at a somewhat higher level. However, learners at *Threshold Level* should be capable of understanding the gist and many relevant details of programmes (e.g. BBC World Service broadcasts) specifically directed to non-native audiences with correspondingly appropriate vocabulary, grammar and pronunciation.

Text types for listening:

Announcements/information through public address systems at bus stations, railway stations, airports, in flight, in discos, stadiums, at pop concerts, etc.; telephone information (e.g. automatic answering devices: weather, traffic conditions, medical services, timetables, etc.); weather forecasts (radio and TV); traffic information (radio); tourist information (e.g. through portable museum guides); publicity texts (radio, TV, supermarket, etc.); routine commands (instructions/directions by police, customs officials, airline personnel, etc.).

Notes

1 All texts should satisfy the final criterion of item 3 of the *extended characterisation* (see Chapter 3).

2 It is in accordance with the nature of the present specification as a general objective that we refrain from including such items as reviews from newspapers and magazines, short stories, poems, comic strips, flow-charts, etc., although it is likely that a learner who has at his disposal the linguistic content of *Threshold Level* would be able to understand much reading material of this kind. In order to meet the needs and interests of particular sub-groups of the target population such items may, of course, be included in specific learning programmes as well as in adaptations of the objective for individual sub-groups.

3 The present specification is the specification of an objective, not of the content of a learning programme. This is why, apart from those listed in the first paragraph of this chapter, no mention is made in this chapter of further techniques that may be usefully employed towards achieving understanding of a text. These techniques, which include segmentation, the establishment of links between segments, underlining, note-taking and note-making, etc., may be profitably practised in a learning programme designed to enable learners to do what is specified in our objective, but they are not presented as components of the objective itself because the extent to which each individual learner makes use of them in satisfying the requirements of the objective is subject to personal variation. In the same way, such strategies as inferencing, hypothesising from proper names, international words, cognate words in the learner's mother tongue or in other languages he or she may have learnt, are all too variable to be specified in a general performance objective. However, an awareness of such techniques and strategies, and experience in their use, form an important aspect of learning to learn (cf. Chapter 13).

10 Writing

The objective for writing at *Threshold Level* is very limited. It is assumed that for this skill the actual needs of the majority of the members of the target group who are expected to be temporary visitors do not go beyond the ability to fill in certain forms, to write a few types of standard letter, and to write simple personal letters on subjects of common interest to themselves and friends or acquaintances. All this falls strictly within items 1 and 2 of the *extended characterisation*. It may be specified as follows:

The learners will be able to complete forms:

- hotel registration forms
- forms required when entering or leaving a foreign country

The learners will be able to write standard letters:

- enquiring about price and conditions of accommodation
- stating wishes as to size of rooms, arrangement (full board, etc.), amenities, view
- enquiring about tourist attractions, sights, etc.
- booking accommodation

The learners will be able to conduct personal correspondence:

- simple messages such as greetings and congratulations
- simple private letters concerning matters of common interest to themselves and friends or acquaintances.

The writing requirements of temporary residents, as set out in the *extended characterisation*, are of a somewhat different character. These learners will almost certainly be called upon to complete a wider range of official forms. They may need to write letters enquiring about accommodation to rent, and if need be, letters of complaint to landlords. They may send written invitations and write brief letters of thanks for hospitality received. They may have to note down and relay messages (e.g. by telephone). They may have to write letters of application for jobs, to report briefly on accidents and complete insurance claims. As parents, they may need to write notes to school explaining a child's absence. In carrying out the above tasks, the learner should be able to observe conventions regarding:

- basic letter layout
- opening and closing formulae (See Language Functions 5.27–28)
- representation of dates (See General Notions 3.3)

- use of capitals and punctuation (, ; : . ! ?)

These tasks can be accomplished within the limits of the resources required for the tasks specified at *Threshold Level*, using the techniques set out in Chapters 12 and 13.

11 Sociocultural competence

Items 4 and 6 of the *extended characterisation* are concerned with 'sociocultural competence', the aspect of communicative ability which involves those specific features of a society and its culture which are manifest in the communicative behaviour of the members of this society. These features may be classified as 'social conventions' (4a), 'social rituals' (4b) and 'universal experiences' (6). The degree of familiarity with them which is required for successful communication depends on the circumstances in which the communication takes place. It will probably be higher in contacts with native speakers of the foreign language (especially when the learner is a temporary resident rather than a visitor) than when the foreign language is used as *lingua franca*. The *Threshold Level* is designed to suit all these types of contacts. This means, on the one hand, that in attempting to indicate what may be expected of a learner at this level we have to focus on the more predictable type of contact, that with native speakers of the foreign language and particularly with such native speakers in their own country. On the other hand it means that an alertness has to be stimulated in the learners to unexpected sociocultural differences between their communication partners and themselves. This applies particularly when English is in use as a medium of international communication between non-native speakers from different cultures. Learners cannot take it for granted that their interlocutor will share either their own values, attitudes, beliefs and social conventions or those of Anglo-Saxon peoples. They will need to be alert to signs of cultural differences, to be tolerant of such differences and be prepared to operate whatever strategies may be needed to establish a proper basis for communication by raising cultural differences into consciousness.

A first approach to a specification of sociocultural competence for *Threshold Level* is to be found in items 4 and 6 of the *extended characterisation*. The formulations chosen there are deliberately open-ended and exemplificatory. This will be the same in the present specification so that it may suit the needs and interests of our highly heterogeneous target population, further concretisations to be undertaken for each sub-group individually. The selection we present below has been made with the utmost economy, taking into account the overall height of the *Threshold Level*.

Parts of the specification of sociocultural competence will correspond to most other components of the *Threshold Level* in that they will describe what the learners can *do* in the foreign language. Other parts, however, will be formulated in terms of the learners' 'awareness of' or 'familiarity with' certain aspects of the foreign culture. An attempt to formulate these parts as well in terms of the learners' behaviour potential would involve choices of such an arbitrary nature that their validity would be unacceptably low. What the specifications in terms of awareness and familiarity are meant to ensure is that at *Threshold Level* the learners will have had certain experiences, that they have been confronted with certain features of the foreign culture and that they have been led to pay attention to them and to try and relate them to their own previous experiences.

In other words, these elements of the *Threshold Level* objective are concerned with learning experiences that the learner is supposed to have had. What the learners do with these experiences and how they affect their own attitudes and behaviour is deliberately left open. This is done to provide the fullest possible scope for the accommodation of the large variety of emphases that will be required for different courses, for different types of learners, and even for individual learners.

Sociocultural competence for English at *Threshold Level*

I   Universal experiences

1   everyday life

The learners have some familiarity with:

- at what times people have their regular meals and in what ways the composition of meals, including beverages, typically differs from that in their own country;
- major national holidays;
- working hours;
- preferred leisure activities (to the extent that generalisation is possible).

2   living conditions

The learners have some familiarity with:

- living standards, including significant differences between major parts of a country;
- ethnic composition of the population.

3   **interpersonal relations**

The learners have some familiarity with:

- class structure of society and relations between the classes;

- relations within the family;

- formality/informality in work situations and in contacts with officials;

- interracial relations;

- major political groups.

4   **major values and attitudes**

The learners have some familiarity with the value generally attached to and the prevalent attitude towards:

- social class;

- wealth and security;

- tradition;

- national identity and foreigners;

- politics;

- religion.

II   **Social conventions and rituals**

1   **non-linguistic**

a) **body language**

The learner is aware of the diversity of conventions in different countries with regard to hand shaking, touching, embracing, kissing, gesticulation, close physical proximity and protracted direct eye contact, and is aware of the embarrassment that may be caused by non-observance of the conventions followed by the interlocutor.

b) **visiting rituals**

The learners know – or can enquire:

- whether they are expected to be punctual;

- whether they are expected to bring a present, and if so what sort of present;

- what sort of clothes to wear;

- whether to expect refreshments, or a meal, if asked for a certain time;
- whether, and how, they are expected to comment on food, furnishings, etc.;
- how long they are expected to stay as well as when and how to take leave.

c eating and drinking rituals

The learners are aware that rituals may differ from what is customary in their own country, and are ready to observe, and if appropriate, follow others' examples.

2 linguistic

The learner is aware of the sociocultural conventions governing the use of the language functions listed in Chapter 5 of this document, and can perform them appropriately. He/she is aware of the conventions of politeness described below and is able to act appropriately in this respect.

In addition to what is specified above, the *Threshold Level* contains a further, implicit, component of sociocultural competence, which is most easily identifiable in the recommended word list. Several items in this list have a meaning which is more or less subtly different from that of their translation equivalents in other languages. For English *tea* is an obvious example, but also such items as *church, soldier, town, vegetables* may not fully correspond in meaning to comparable words in other languages. At *Threshold Level* the learner cannot be expected to be aware of all these differences, except to the extent that awareness of them is essential to successful communication within the contexts listed under items 1 and 2 of the *extended characterisation*.

Politeness conventions

The exponents recommended for use at *Threshold Level*, even more so for *Waystage*, are generally of a simple and direct nature. As such, they will be readily understood by other language users. However, they are sometimes open to misinterpretation as showing insufficient regard for the feelings of the partner and thus lacking in politeness. One way to avoid this impression is by smiling, making eye contact and generally signalling goodwill through body language. Learners should, however, also be aware of the main features of politeness in speech so as to recognise them in the speech of others and respond appropriately, and also to follow the same principles in their own speech as they feel to be appropriate to the situation and their relation to the partner. In some cases, the use of a politeness marker is so usual that we have included it directly in the suggested exponent. However, to have attempted to do so in all cases would have both overloaded the specification and been in fact too directive and even misleading. We have preferred to state the principles and to leave it to learners, under guidance from their teachers, to apply them appropriately.

The basic principle of politeness is to show respect for the partner. In particular, the speaker tries to avoid embarrassment, distress or displeasure by showing an awareness of the demands made upon the partner by what he/she says. In this way the possibility of overt conflict is avoided or reduced. The principle can be embodied in a number of maxims:

1 *Do not be dogmatic.* Remember that the partner may have a different opinion.
   This maxim applies to the functions of imparting factual information and expressing attitudes. It implies qualifying simple declarative sentences in the following ways:

   a) the use of *I think, I believe, I expect,* as introducers or as tags. If they are unstressed, their use does not indicate uncertainty or lack of confidence;
   I ·think his 'mother is I͵talian.
   She ·comes from Ca⌐labria, I be·lieve.

   b) the use of *you know, of course,* to imply that the partner is not ignorant;
   Of ·course, his 'mother is I͵talian, you ·know.

   c) the use of tag questions to invite the partner's agreement (falling intonation) or confirmation (rising intonation).
   His 'mother is I⌐talian, | ⌐isn't she? **(inviting agreement; no uncertainty);**
   His 'mother is I⌐talian, | ͵isn't she? **(asking confirmation; uncertain).**

Correcting is liable to give offence, since it involves telling the partner that he/she has made a mistake. Offence can be avoided by:

- **apologising for correcting;**
  I'm ˇsorry, | but the ·lecture 'isn't on ˇWednesday. | It's on ⌐Friday.

- **querying what has been said, so that the partner can correct the slip;**
  'Blue? 'Did you ·say her ·dress was ͵blue?

- **presenting the correction as a different opinion;**
  'Fifty-'four? | I ·thought ·eight ·sevens were 'fifty-⌐six.

- **requesting confirmation by the use of a question tag.**
  Nicaˇragua? | San Jo·se is in ͵Costa ⌐Rica, | ͵isn't it?

2 *Be reluctant to say what may distress or displease the partner.* This applies to such functions as breaking bad news, expressing disagreement,

declining offers and invitations, saying that the partner is obliged to do something, prohibiting and withholding permission, expressing displeasure, dislike, dissatisfaction, disappointment and disapproval. The maxim implies such strategies as:

a) expressing reluctance;

I 'don't ·want to com^{v}plain | but, ... (e.g. this ·soup is 'cold).

I 'don't ·want to be ^{v}difficult | but ... (e.g. this ma·chine doesn't 'work).

I 'don't ·like ^{v}saying so, | but ... (e.g. the ·music is 'too ˌloud).

b) seeking the partner's agreement;

I 'hope you ·don't ·mind me ^{v}saying so, | but ... (e.g. 'those 'colours ·don't ˌmix).

'Don't you aˌgree | that ... (e.g. 'that ·colour is ·rather too ˌbright).

c) apologising or expressing regret;

I'm ^{v}sorry, | but ... (e.g. your 'work is ·not ˌgood e·nough).

I'm a·fraid ... (e.g. you 'haven't ·passed your eˌxam).

This is especially frequent in prohibitions and withholding permission.

I'm ^{v}sorry, | but you 'can't ·leave to^{v}morrow.

I'm a·fraid you 'can't ·smoke in ^{v}here.

d) using euphemisms;

e.g. Your ·work 'isn't ·very ^{v}good ... (= your work is bad).

I 'can't ·say I ^{v}like it ... (= I dislike it).

e) implying something unpleasant rather than stating it openly.

e.g. I'd ^{v}like to ·help you ... (implying but I can't).

Your i·deas are ^{v} interesting ... (implying but I don't agree with them).

Note the frequent use of falling–rising intonations.

Expressing disagreement is likely to cause offence and to lead to conflict. The risk can be reduced by:

- apologising for not agreeing;
  e.g. I'm ^{v}sorry, | but I 'don't aˌgree.

- expressing regret for not agreeing.
  e.g. I'm a·fraid that 'isn't ˌtrue.

3 *Do not force the partner to act.* Allow him/her to appear to act voluntarily. This maxim applies to the functions of suasion, seeking factual information and finding out attitudes. It implies:

a) adding *please* when you call for action by the partner;
  i) 'Where is the ˌtoilet, ·please?   (asking for information);
  ii) A reˈturn ·ticket to ˌLondon, ·please. (requesting something);
  iii) 'Sit ˌdown, ·please.   (giving instructions, orders).

b) avoiding simple imperatives when asking the partner to do something for you. Instead,
  i) ask if he/she
      is willing to act,   e.g. 'Will you ·open the ˌwindow, ·please?
      is able to act,   e.g. 'Can you ·open this ˌtin for me, ·please?
      wishes to act.   e.g. 'Would you ·like to ˌhelp me, ·please?

  ii) use introducers such as
      I wonder if ...   e.g. I 'wonder if you could ·close the ˌwindow, ·please?
      Do you think ...   e.g. 'Do you ·think you could ·open this ˌtin for me, ·please?

  iii) use warnings or advice
      e.g. 'Don't for·get to ·post the ˅letter.
            If ˅I were ·you, | I'd 'keep your 'eyes on the ˋroad.

  iv) draw attention to the situation, inviting the partner to recognise that there is a problem that needs to be dealt with.
      e.g. It's ˋcold in ·here, | ˋisn't it? (= please close the window).
            I 'can't ·open this ˌtin.   (= please open it for me).
            'Dinner's ˌready.   (= come and sit down to eat it).

Asking is a form of suasion, since the partner is asked to do something for you, namely provide information. *Wh* questions are normally accompanied by 'please'. After the partner has replied it is normal to thank him/her for doing so.

'What's the ˌtime, ·please?

'Twelve o'ˌclock.

ˌThank you.

Offers and invitations are very much subject to politeness conventions, but in a complex way, since they attempt to persuade the partner to act in a certain way, but in the interests of the partner rather than of the speaker. Invitations and offers may be strong or weak.

A 'strong' offer or invitation, making it easier for the partner to accept, may be conveyed:

• by using an imperative as though it were an order;
  e.g. 'Let me ˌhelp you.
        'Give ˌme that ·case to ·carry.
        'Come and ·spend the ·day in ˌOxford.

- by expressing obligation or necessity;
  e.g. You 'must let ˌme ·carry that ·case.
- by demanding a promise;
  e.g. 'Promise you will ·come to ˌdinner with us.
- by demanding confirmation of an imputed intention.
  e.g. You ˌwill be our ˌguests, | ˌwon't you?

Note the use of low falling intonations with strong offers and invitations.

A 'weak' offer or invitation makes it possible for the partner to decline:

- by using an interrogative question regarding the partner's intentions, desires, needs or ability.
  e.g. 'Are you ·coming to ˌdinner?
  'Would you ·like some ˌhelp with that ·problem?
  'Do you ·need any ˌhelp?
  'Can you ·come to ·dinner next ˌWednesday?

Especially weak are offers that:

a) require the partner to admit that he/she is unable to refuse;

  e.g. 'Can you ˌmanage?
  'Are you ˌstuck?

b) are negatively phrased.

  e.g. I 'don't sup·pose you could ·do with some ˅help?
  'You 'don't re·quire asˌsistance, | ˌdo you?

Note the prevalence of rising intonation with weak offers. Strong offers can be accepted without demur, or confirmation can be invited:

  e.g. 'Are you ˌsure?
  'Is ·that ·all ˌright?

A weak offer or invitation is not usually accepted without demur. More commonly, a repeated offer is invited:

  e.g. 'Won't that be ·too much ˌtrouble?
  'Can you ·spare the ˌtime?
  It's very 'heavy, | ·that ˌcase.

or a weak rejection is offered:

  e.g. 'No, ˌthank you, | I 'don't want to ˅bother you.
  I'm ·sure you're 'much ·too ·busy.

This allows the partner to withdraw the offer or invitation:

e.g. 'Well, | as a 'matter of ˅fact, | I 'am ·rather ˌbusy.
  ˌRight ·then. | So 'long as you can ˌmanage.

or to repeat it, usually in a stronger form:

e.g. ˋNo, | ˋreally. | I'd ˋlike to ·help.
ˋNo, | ˋdo ·come. | We'd 'very ·much ˋlike you to ·come.

The declining of a strong invitation is usually accompanied by an apology, or a reason for declining an offer:

e.g. ·Well, ˋthank you, | but I'm ˇsorry, | I'm a·fraid I have a'nother en˷gagement.
'No ˎthank you, | I 'don't ˎsmoke.
ˎThanks, | but it's 'easier by my˷self.

A suggestion for further contact, or even an invitation to visit, may be a polite or a well-intentioned way of ending a contact. Its formal acceptance need not entail a firm commitment on either side:

e.g. **A:** 'Do ˎvisit us ·next ·time you're in ·London.
B: ˋThank you, | I ˋwill.

Apologies are often called for in social life, for reasons ranging from the trivial and conventional to serious damage or inconvenience. For brushing against someone in passing a perfunctory apology is sufficient:

e.g. ˇSorry.

On the other hand, if damage or inconvenience are caused, as when you keep someone waiting for an appreciable time, the apology normally involves an explanation:

e.g. I'm 'very ·sorry | to ·be so ˎlate. || I'm a·fraid I 'missed the ˎtrain.

The politeness conventions described above are widely used and understood in English-speaking countries, especially between speakers in the roles characteristic of *Threshold Level*. A learner at *Threshold Level* should be able to recognise their use and to identify the attitudes and intentions of speakers who use them. Their appropriate use is, however, governed by such factors as:

- the social and regional groups to which the speaker belongs. There are differences in usage between men and women, working and middle class, the North and South of Britain, etc.;

- the speaker's personality: some people are more direct, others more sensitive to the feelings of other people;

- the relations of the conversational partners: close friends need make less use of politeness conventions than acquaintances or strangers;

- the nature of the situation: urgent emergencies demand immediate decisive action. Where conflicts of interest arise and polite methods fail, a learner may well need to be frank, even blunt in speaking his/her mind.

12 Compensation strategies

No matter how hard we try to assess and to predict learners' communication needs, to determine the situations requiring foreign language use which they are most likely to find themselves in, and to identify those language forms which are most likely to enable them to cope with these situations, there will always be a very broad margin of unpredictability. And even if the demands of a particular communication situation do not exceed that which the learners have been thoroughly prepared for, there are likely to be failures of recall, failures to activate, on the spur of the moment, certain items of knowledge or elements of skill that were acquired during the learning process.

This means that even if we confine ourselves to the requirements of everyday situations, unpredictable to a certain extent, the learner has to be prepared to cope with unpredicted demands as well as with failures of recall.

To some people skill in coping comes naturally. Somehow they manage, whatever their lack of skill or knowledge with regard to the 'proper' form of communication. Most people, however, will benefit substantially by being given ample opportunity, in the course of their learning process, to develop their skill in this respect. It is not primarily a matter of being 'taught' how to cope, but of being led to develop one's own strategies for doing so. Although certain strategies and techniques may almost certainly be beneficial to everyone, individual differences corresponding to differences in personality are to be given full scope.

What may be expected of learners at *Threshold Level*, then, is some skill in dealing with the demands of a communication situation that they are not fully prepared for. This means particularly that:

as a reader or listener the learner is not 'thrown' by the occurrence of unknown linguistic elements in a text;

as a speaker or writer the learner is prepared to seek solutions to problems caused by insufficient linguistic skill or knowledge;

as a social agent the learner is not put out by uncertainty as to the accepted code of behaviour.

There is no direct relationship between these attitudinal aspects and specific abilities. Different learners are likely to develop different sets of strategies for coping with the problems involved. Consequently, no standard operationalisation is to be sought. Yet, among the various techniques and strategies that are available a certain number may be identified as particularly likely to suit each individual learner and to contribute substantially to the development of the desired attitudes.

Like other aspects of communicative ability at *Threshold Level*, this may be described and listed in terms of what the learner can do, and supplemented with recommended exponents where this is appropriate. Because some items will require the fulfilling of particular language functions and the handling of particular notions, a partial overlap with other lists in the present objective is inevitable. A similar overlap will occur between the present list and that of the chapter on 'dealing with texts' (Chapter 9).

I   **As a reader**, the learner can:

1 deduce the meanings of complex words composed of elements (base(s) and affixes) which are familiar to the learner and which are combined in accordance with productive rules of word formation, insofar as these meanings are directly derivable on the basis of familiarity with the elements involved and with generally applied rules of word formation;

2 deduce the meanings of unfamiliar elements (particularly phrases and words) from a context of familiar elements which allows these meanings to be identified;

3 correctly interpret the meanings of so-called 'international words' that are familiar from the learner's native language and whose formal relation to the native language equivalent is fully transparent; he/she is aware of the existence of 'false friends' and will remain on the alert for differences in the meanings of 'international' words and cognate words from one language to another;

4 find the meanings of unknown words or phrases in a bilingual dictionary or alphabetically arranged word list as well as in a monolingual dictionary, provided that the defining vocabulary contains mostly familiar elements;

5 with or without the aid of the above devices derive specific information from a text containing unknown elements, provided that, in addition to what is specified elsewhere in the present objective, this does not require further abilities than those listed above, the acceptable degree of difficulty of the text depending on the availability or non-availability of a dictionary or word list.

II   **As a listener**, the learner can:

1 carry out the operation described in I.1, provided that the word-formation process involved does not entail further phonological changes in the constituent elements than linking, stress adjustment, and consequent (regular) vowel and consonant changes;

2 carry out the operation described in I.2, provided that the contextual clues are presented in such a way that they are recognisable as such and interpretable in linear sequence without necessitating backtracking and reconsideration of the context;

3 carry out the operation described in I.3, provided that phonological differences between the foreign language form and the native language form are confined to standard correspondences between the two languages;

4 derive specific information from a text containing unknown elements, provided that, in addition to what is specified elsewhere in the present objective, this does not require further abilities than those listed in II.1, II.2 and II.3;

5 in face-to-face contacts appeal to a communication partner's assistance, particularly by using the devices listed in section 6 of Language Functions.

III   **As a speaker**, the learner can:

1 introduce a rephrasing
(˅Sorry,) I'll 'start a͵gain.
(˅Sorry,) I'll 'try to ·say that a͵gain.

2 describe by means of paraphrase, particularly by using a general word (*person, thing*, etc.) or a superordinate, together with a qualification indicating:
• general physical properties such as colour, size, shape (See General Notions.)
• specific features **(an X with three legs)**
• use **(an X to cut bread)**

3 describe by referring to qualities and properties:
• general physical properties (See General Notions.)
It is ...
• specific features
It has ...
• use
You can ... with it.

4 identify by indicating
one ·like ͵that.
I'd ·like ͵this, ·please.

5 appeal for assistance
'What do you ͵call ·that (a·gain)?
I 'don't ·know the ·English/·German, **etc.** ͵word.
In [native language] we say ...

IV   **As a writer**, the learner can:

1 express ignorance
   I 'don't ·know ·how to ˌsay it.
   I 'don't ·know ·what you ˌcall it.

2 use the devices mentioned under III.2 and III.3;

3 use dictionaries, both bilingual and monolingual of an appropriate kind.

V   **As a social agent**, the learner can:

1 apologise for uncertainty or ignorance as to the accepted code of behaviour
   I'm ˇsorry | I 'don't/ˈdidn't ˈknow ...

2 refer to what is customary in his/her own country
   In ˇmy ·country we ...

3 ask for guidance
   'How is this ˌdone in ·your ·country?
   'How should I ˌdo this?
   'What should I ˌdo?
   At 'what ·time should I ˌcome?
   etc.

The above strategies and techniques are those that every learner at *Threshold Level* may be expected to be able to use together with the use of the language functions listed in section 6 of Chapter 5. In addition, each individual learner is likely to have other privileged devices at his or her disposal. They may, but will not necessarily, include such techniques as finding information in grammatical surveys, in general reference works, etc., and such strategies as using a synonym for an unknown word, allowing oneself to use grammatically imperfect forms, experimenting with word formation, foreignising a native-language form, etc. Which of these devices the learners are given opportunities to adopt cannot be laid down in a general objective but is to be left to those providing learning facilities.

13 Learning to learn

The *Threshold Level* is an objective derived from the estimated needs of the learners or communicators. A course – that is the sum total of the learning experiences offered to the learners – designed for *Threshold Level* will have to enable the learners to satisfy these needs. Yet, it will inevitably do other things as well. Depending on its design and presentation it may give the learners pleasure or hardship, it may promote, maintain, or reduce their motivation for learning, it may bolster or diminish their self-confidence, it may stimulate their interest and sensitivity to the world around them or it may cause them to withdraw into themselves; in short, it may benefit the learners far beyond the basic objectives of the course or it may limit itself to these and, possibly, it may even harm the learners as persons. All these effects – positive or negative – are independent of the learning load that is represented by the content of an objective, they are produced by the impact upon particular learners of the forms and the manners of the presentation and the practice of this content. At the same time they may affect the learners' impression of the learning load in making this load appear to be more demanding or less so.

The experience, then, of learning for *Threshold Level* will affect the learners in various ways beyond the acquisition of a certain learning content. One of the ways in which it may substantially benefit the learners is in stimulating their awareness of the learning process itself and increasing their learning potential. This 'learning to learn' does not, at first sight, appear to fall within our communicative objective. It may, however, easily be integrated into this objective. And there are at least two good reasons for trying to do so. In the first place, it has now long been accepted by learning psychologists that insightful learning is likely to be more effective – and to produce more lasting effects – than learning without insight. This greater effectiveness is partly due to the motivating power of knowing what one is doing and why one is doing it. Secondly, 'learning to learn' is an invaluable aspect of preparing the learners for whatever further learning may be required by them. Like any general objective, the *Threshold Level* is no more than an assessment of what the average member of a particular target group is most likely to need at a given stage in his or her development. The actual needs of individual members of the target group are certain to differ to a greater or a lesser extent from those of the fictitious 'average member'. This means that in order to be adequately equipped for independent functioning in and with the foreign language, learners should have the insights and know-how required for bridging the gap between their individual needs and those provided for in the specifications of the general objective. And even if the gap is so wide that the learners may have to seek professional guidance, some insight into their own learning potential and how to exploit this most effectively will be of considerable advantage to them.

Finally it should be said that the promotion of learner autonomy is a fundamental objective of the communicative approach adopted by the Council of Europe. That is to say the learners should be encouraged and enabled to take increasing charge of their own learning and to develop the attitudes, knowledge, understanding and skills which will enable them to do so. Insofar as the *Threshold Level* is the statement of a learning objective and not just a description of a certain level of proficiency, the skills involved in learning to learn are not simply a by-product of some courses, but an essential aspect of that objective, which all teaching towards that objective should promote. As such they form an integral part of the objective, not an optional extra.

Thus, in describing what learners should be able to do with and through the use of language for communication, we legitimately take into account their use of the experience of language learning to become more efficient and effective language learners as well as language users. It is part of the *Threshold Level* objectives for learners to be willing and able to engage in the struggle to communicate in the situations confronting them with the resources and strategies they command, taking the risk of error, inviting and welcoming various forms of assistance from more experienced interlocutors and, systematically, to learn from the experience. It is also part of the objective that learners should actively seek opportunities for engaging in such encounters, exploiting not only the presence of native speakers in the environment but also the opportunities offered by radio and television broadcasts as well as printed and recorded material.

'Learning to learn', as we said above, should be incorporated into the *Threshold Level* objective, not as an additional objective that will affect the pragmatic/linguistic content but as one that is to be achieved through the form and manner of presentation and practice of this content or, indeed, through the individual's experience of the language. We shall formulate the learning-to-learn component in terms of a learning objective, but at a fairly high level of generality, leaving scope for a range of concrete realisations by individual learners with possibly different learning styles.

The 'learning-to-learn' objective

I Concerning needs and objectives

1 The learners are aware of the nature of their communicative needs.

2 The learners are aware of the nature of the learning objective offered to them.

3 The learners have insight into the degree of relevance to their communicative needs of the learning objective offered to them.

4 In the areas covered by the open categories of Chapter 7 (Specific notions) the learners are able to identify, learn and use the terms specific to their own nationality, employment, leisure interests, etc.

5 The learners can identify those of their communicative needs, if any, which are not catered for in the objective offered to them.

6 The learners can describe, in general terms, additional objectives which will satisfy the needs referred to under 5 above and/or they can recognise the relevance to those needs of further objectives offered to them, for example:

I'd 'like to ·read ·articles about eco,nomics.
I'd 'like to ·write ˌbusiness ·letters.

II Concerning learning processes

1 The learners are familiar with the possibility of dividing an overall learning task into a number of sub-tasks, each with its own objective.

2 The learners are familiar with the distinction between productive ability and receptive ability and with the difference in degree of skill that may be required in order to meet the needs for each type of ability.

3 The learners are aware of the contributions of pragmatic, grammatical, lexical and phonological adequacy to communicative effectiveness.

4 The learners can identify the roles (acquisition of knowledge, of insight, of skill) of various types of learning materials and are aware of the potential relevance of such materials to the achievement of their objective.

5 The learners know how to find information about usage (e.g. in dictionaries, relevant reference works and reference grammars designed for use by non-advanced learners).

6 The learners have experienced various methods of vocabulary acquisition and have identified one or more that they consider particularly useful to themselves.

7 The learners are aware of the potential of learning through exposure to foreign language use and know how various compensation strategies may enable them to cope with texts containing unknown elements (cf. Chapter 9, note 3).

III Concerning learning from direct experience of the language

1 The learners are able to engage in communicative interaction using the resources and strategies specified at *Threshold Level* and to learn from experience.

2 The learners are able to observe the language and strategies used by a more experienced interlocutor and thus increase their own repertory of responses, receptive and productive.

3 The learners are, for instance, able as listeners and as readers to perceive, memorise and note down words and expressions not previously encountered, noting also their situational context and functional/notional value.

4 The learners are able to repeat back new words and expressions which occur in conversations in which they participate, to make use of them themselves as soon as appropriate and, by later making notes if necessary, add them to their repertory.

5 The learners are able to experiment with forms of expression (e.g. by re-combining known words and grammatical structures, or rules of word and structure formation), to note their acceptance or non-acceptance by more experienced speakers and, if need be, to modify the rules they operate.

6 The learners are able to employ compensation and repair strategies (cf. section 6 of Chapter 5), noting, learning and using new language supplied by their interlocutor.

IV Concerning evaluation

1 The learners can monitor their progress towards the terminal objective particularly by relating their communicative ability to successive intermediate objectives.

2 The learners are aware of the role of formative assessment as an aid to the planning of further learning activities.

The above analysis of 'learning to learn' is based on assumptions as to what may reasonably be expected to be feasible for learners at an early stage of foreign language learning without diverting too much of their attention from the actual task of learning to use the language itself.

Some learners may well find further items useful, such as ability to consult a reference grammar designed for use by non-advanced foreign learners. It is for the student, preferably with the advice of the teacher, to decide whether its use would facilitate learning at this level or require an expenditure of time and energy incommensurate with the modest requirements of the *Threshold Level* objective itself.

Several of the above items are formulated as 'the learners are aware of ...'. This obviously allows for different degrees of awareness, and no attempt is made to operationalise this concept. This simply means that, in our view, courses meant to lead up to *Threshold Level* should provide learners with the opportunity to develop the awareness concerned without, however, making any specific demands upon the learners in this respect.

14 Degree of skill

So far, in the present study, we have been concerned with what learners might have to be able to do in the foreign language in order to satisfy their needs and interests. What we have not dealt with is *how* they should be able to do all the things specified. We have – it is true – listed many exponents (language forms) and strategies that, together, might enable the learners to function economically and effectively in the situations they are most likely to find themselves in. However, the exponents have been offered merely by way of recommendation and the strategies have mostly been described in an open-ended manner.

All this is tantamount to saying that the level we have described is not uniform and fixed but that it allows of many different concretisations in accordance with the diversity of sub-groups and individual members of the target population. Consequently, it is not in itself either a testing syllabus or a course design. However, its high degree of explicitness allows it to be used as a basis for these. A test syllabus designer will then have to determine the exact nature of the concretisations that correspond to the purposes of the text envisaged and thus establish the criteria the learners will have to satisfy in order to pass the test.

Threshold Level 1990, then, is simply a learning objective, an aim to be pursued with and by the learners and which is specified in such a way that it can give meaningful direction to the planning of learning activities. It is not to be confused with actual learning effects. These will always differ from what is described in an objective. The extent of the difference that is acceptable is primarily a matter for individual learners to decide in accordance with their own needs and ambitions.

Consequently, in dealing with the question *how* and particularly *how well* the learners should be able to do what is specified in this objective we cannot go beyond very general statements which mainly concern minimal requirements for effective communication.

An attempt at communication is effective if the intention of a communicative act is realised. This is the case if the communicator is successful in conveying his or her intention to others and also in correctly interpreting others' intentions that may be relevant to his or her own situation. This means that the main criterion to be applied is *pragmatic adequacy*. If a learner means to apologise humbly or to express doubt he/she communicates effectively if a communication partner understands that he or she is apologising humbly or expressing doubt. And if a learner wants to find out whether or not to wear a raincoat he/she is an effective communicator if he/she correctly interprets the relevant information in a weather forecast.

However, we should not jump to the conclusion that a learner who communicates successfully on one particular occasion has established his or her credentials as a good communicator and has reached the *Threshold Level* objective. Under favourable circumstances (a constraining situation and an alert, experienced and sympathetic native listener) communication may be unaffected by even gross phonetic, grammatical and lexical distortion. Speech recognition experiments show the great effect of the listener's expectations on identification. The same utterance may well fail to communicate under less constraining circumstances (if, say, the referent is unobservable and not deducible from context) or if the listener is less motivated or less experienced. In particular, non-native listeners are less able to cope with deviance than native speakers. This point is of particular relevance when English is used as a means of communication between non-native speakers of different mother tongues. A level of mother tongue interference which does not interfere seriously with communication with native speakers or with others who have the same mother tongue background may make conversation impossible, or lead to misunderstandings with serious consequences (e.g. where safety or security are involved) where the listener has to rely on the accurate identification of what has been said.

Thus, verbal communication cannot be reasonably assured without at least an approximation to certain grammatical, lexical and phonological norms. This means that errors in these areas that interfere with communicative effectiveness are not acceptable. This conclusion does not, however, automatically lead to the establishment of lists of acceptable and unacceptable deviations from norms.

By definition, any failure to distinguish phonemic pairs, or grammatical categories (e.g. tense/aspect distinctions), is capable of leading to misunderstanding, but the factors which decide whether or not it does so are so complex as to defy quantification. In a high proportion of cases listeners (especially native listeners) will be aware that the speech is deviant, but will understand what the speaker intends. Whether or not such errors are accepted in an otherwise successful communicative act depends on other considerations than those inherent in the present objective. Largely, this is a matter of the learners' personalities and their ambitions. A naturally shy person may be severely handicapped as a communicator by being conscious of frequently producing incorrect forms. And one who needs full acceptance as a communication partner in an environment that is intolerant of any manifestation of reduced competence will also need a higher degree of skill than many other learners. The *Threshold Level*, as specified in this document, does not in any way preclude the development of such a higher degree of skill but it does not require it of all the learners within its target group.

Yet it will be to all learners' advantage to set their sights a little higher than just 'pragmatic adequacy'. They should also aim at the ability to communicate with a certain degree of *efficiency*. Speakers who, when giving information about something, have to pause after every second word in order to find a way to continue, who make numerous grammatical and/or lexical mistakes even in short utterances, whose pronunciation does not conform to any standard their communication partner may be familiar with, etc., cannot be said to communicate efficiently because they put a great strain on those listening to them and run the risk of losing their audience altogether.

There is a similar lack of efficiency when listeners, in order to understand what is said to them, need constant repetition or oblige speakers to speak with unnatural slowness or to rephrase their sentences all the time so as to express themselves within an inadequately narrow range of vocabulary and grammar. It may be expected then, at *Threshold Level*, that, within the limits set by *Threshold Level* content:

- *as speakers* the learners can make themselves easily understood not only by listeners with native or near-native command of the language, but also under normal conditions by other non-native speakers who have reached *Threshold Level*;

- *as listeners* the learners can understand the essence of what is said to them not only by speakers with native or near-native command of the language, but also under normal conditions by other non-native speakers who have reached *Threshold Level*, without obliging the speakers to exert themselves unduly.

What was said of the learners as speakers will equally apply to the learners as writers. As writers, however, the learners are likely to wish to satisfy somewhat higher criteria of formal correctness, particularly in letters to strangers. Having access to appropriate reference works will enable them to satisfy such criteria more easily than in the production of spoken language.

In all that is said above with regard to efficiency of communication it is to be understood that a certain tolerance and co-operation is expected of the learners' communication partners. It would be unrealistic to assume that at *Threshold Level* the learners would be able to function adequately without this. Ability to function in more demanding situations as well does not necessarily require further learning efforts but will develop gradually as learners use the language in practice.

Appendix A Pronunciation and intonation

Communication depends upon mutual intelligibility. That is to say that it is only possible if the language forms produced by the speaker are identified and understood by the listener. It is therefore the responsibility of speakers to pronounce them as *intelligibly* as possible, and it is also the responsibility of listeners actively to seek to identify what has been said and to use appropriate repair procedures if they are unable to do so. The ease of communication depends largely on the extent to which speaker and listener share a common practice. Speakers of the same dialect understand each other without difficulty, but widely separated dialects may well be mutually unintelligible. For purposes of national (or international) communication standard languages with standard pronunciations have generally developed, based usually on the speech of educated people in capital cities, or that of some other prestigious social group. The standard language is widely used in the education system, in the serious media and in middle-class life and culture. This is not to say that all users of a standard pronunciation sound alike. The speaker's socio-regional provenance may be clearly marked and easily detectable by an experienced listener. It may well be important to the individual's sense of identity that this should be so (e.g. Scottish English), but conformity to national norms is sufficient to ensure ready mutual intelligibility on a national scale. In Britain, this role is played by Received Pronunciation (RP) as codified by D. Jones, A. C. Gimson and others, and generally adoped by broadcasting authorities, dictionary makers, language course designers, etc. In its pure form, RP is the practice of a small but influential minority, but with increasing mobility and media exposure a high proportion of speakers use, either habitually or as required, a regionally-coloured approximation to RP which is universally intelligible. Regional variants differ mainly in vowel colouring. The consonant system (which has been shown to play the larger role in identifying speech) is relatively uniform and stable.

On a global scale, English is polycentric. There is no one form of English universally accepted as authoritative. Ireland, the USA, Canada and Australia have their own norms, each related to standard written English and to spoken dialectical variation in much the same way as RP. These norms are fully mutually intelligible and acceptable. All are products of the modern period and have undergone no major sound changes. There is increasingly frequent communication among the communities involved. In countries where English is not the native language, the British norm predominates in educational systems in countries which have recently become independent (India, Africa) and more generally in Europe. The General American norm predominates in the Americas and is widely used in the entertainments industry and in industrial management, in which areas it has considerable influence on British usage. Those (e.g. teachers) who have spent a considerable period in one or another English-speaking country are, of course, likely to have learned to conform to its linguistic norms.

At the present time it seems reasonable in a European context to continue (as in the case of Spanish and French) to adhere to the norms of the European rather than the American variety.

At *Threshold Level*, learners should be able:

- as listeners, to identify the words and expressions used by native speakers of the (regionally coloured) standard variants of English (RP, Polite Scottish, Irish, General American and Australian) and by non-native speakers whose speech, though also regionally coloured, approximates to those norms;

- as speakers, to produce spoken English which is readily intelligible both to native speakers and to non-native speakers who approximate to standard norms.

Among the implications of these objectives are:

- learners should be given experience in listening to a variety of norms, and/or regionally coloured speech (including the principal non-native varieties) which approximate to those norms and remain fully intelligible;

- learners should target one of the native norms (which in a European context may well be British RP), but should not be required or expected to approximate to it more closely than is required for full intelligibility, not only to native English speakers, but also to other non-native learners who have reached *Threshold Level*.

Accordingly, learners at *Threshold Level* should be aware of the pronunciation in RP of the words and expressions proposed as exponents. That is to say:

- they will be aware of the relation between the sound and spelling of English words, avoiding simple orthoepic errors;

- they will be aware of and preserve in their own speech the vowel and, particularly, consonant contrasts of the English model they adopt;

- they will be aware of and preserve in their own speech the placement of stress in polysyllabic words;

- they will be able to distinguish by ear non-homophonous English words and expressions;

- they will be aware of some of the principal meaningful contrasts in utterances carried by stress placement and intonation and will be able to recognise and understand them in the speech of others;

- they will be aware of the principal respects in which the accent of learners with their mother tongue background deviates from RP in ways which are likely to impede recognition and thus communication.

Some form of phonetic transcription conforming to the principles of the International Phonetic Association (IPA), e.g. that used in D. Jones: *An English Pronouncing Dictionary*) (14th edn. ed. A. C. Gimson) or in one of the major monolingual or bilingual dictionaries may be found useful for raising awareness and for reference purposes, but does not in itself constitute part of the *Threshold Level* objective.

Intonation

The intonation of English (RP) is described in detail in such works as G. F. Arnold and J. D. O'Connor: *The Intonation of Colloquial English*. It is used by native speakers on the one hand to indicate the informational structure of sentences and on the other to express nuances of meaning, to indicate unspoken implications or reservations and to convey attitudes and emotional states. As such it plays a very important part in communication and is a frequent source of intercultural misunderstandings. Learners at *Threshold Level* should recognise and understand the most common intonations used in RP for such purposes. In their own speech they should organise the phrasing, stressing and rhythm of tone groups in accordance with RP norms, and employ rising and falling nuclei appropriately.

Where language forms are cited in this book (e.g. as exponents of language functions or examples of grammatical or lexical entries) the most common intonation pattern (not always the only one possible) is shown in accordance with the conventions shown below. These conventions are similar, but not identical, to those used by Arnold and O'Connor.

A full treatment of English intonation is beyond the scope of this book. The most important features at *Threshold Level* are tone groups. For the most part, learners at *Threshold Level* will express themselves in fairly short simple sentences, each consisting of a single tone group. Within the tone group, stressed syllables are spoken in a regular rhythm, unstressed syllables being made to fit in between the beats. The stressed syllables of words which convey lexical information (mainly nouns, adjectives, principal verbs and adverbs) are given prominence in the intonation pattern, unless the information has already been mentioned or is obvious in context. In that case, whilst continuing to mark the rhythmic beat, they are not given pitch prominence. At

Threshold Level, two points of pitch prominence are of importance, the *nucleus* and the *head*. The last prominent stressed syllable in a tone group is its *nucleus*, which initiates a pitch pattern which continues to the end of the tone group, including any unstressed or stressed but non-prominent syllables that follow. The pattern used is closely related to the language function of the sentence and its grammatical category. At *Threshold Level*, five nuclear tones should be distinguished:

1 *Low falling* This is marked by a left to right diagonal falling mark, below the line of writing, placed before the nuclear syllable [ˌ]. This mark is to be interpreted as indicating that the next syllable is stressed. Its vowel starts on a clear, level low-mid tone. The voice then drops to a low creaky note and remains on this low pitch until the end of the tone group.

2 *High falling* This is similar to the low fall, except that the nuclear vowel starts on a pitch above the mid point. It is marked by placing the mark above the line of writing [ˈ].

3 *Low rising* This is marked by a rising mark placed before the nuclear syllable and below the line of writing [ˌ]. It indicates that the next syllable is stressed. Its vowel starts on a clear, low level pitch. There is then a continuous glide upward, but not rising above mid, until the end of the tone group. The glide occurs within the nuclear syllable if it is the last in the group. If it is followed by one or more non-prominent syllables (the 'tail'), stressed or unstressed, the nuclear syllable is spoken on a low level pitch and the rise spans the tail.

4 *High rising* This is shown by placing the rising mark above the line of writing [ˈ]. It indicates that the nuclear vowel starts somewhere between low and mid-level, and that the upward glide extends well above mid.

5 *Falling rising* This may be seen as a sequence of 2 and 3. The nuclear vowel sound starts high-mid pitch and drops to a low creak. An upward glide follows, which does not go above mid. This tone is indicated by a v-shaped mark placed before the nuclear syllable above the line of writing [ˇ]. *Threshold Level* learners should be made aware of the following uses of nuclear tones and be stimulated to use them themselves as appropriate.

1 *Low falling* [ˌ] is used

a) in declarative sentences

    i) for factual statements e.g. identifying, defining, describing and narrating as well as in answers to *wh* questions (which may be short phrases or single words);
    'This is a ˌdoor. They 'drove to ˌLondon. 'Dogs are ˌanimals.

    ii) for expressing definite agreement or disagreement, firm denials, firm acceptance or rejection of an offer, definite statements of intention, obligation, granting or withholding permission, etc. In general, it indicates an unambiguous certainty.

That's 'quite ˌright. You 'must ·eat your ˌdinner.

b) in interrogative sentences answerable by *yes* or *no*

i) in interrogation, to indicate that an answer is demanded;

'Have you ·seen this ·man beˌfore?

ii) in requests to indicate that they are in effect orders;

'May I ·see your ˌdriving ·licence, ·please? ·Will you 'please be ˌquiet.

iii) when a series of *yes/no* questions is posed in rapid succession;

'Is it ˌred? 'Can you ˌeat it? 'Is it a ˌcabbage?

iv) in tag questions, to invite agreement to a statement that is not in doubt;

'This ·tastes ˌnice, | ˌdoesn't it?

v) in choice questions, to indicate that the list of options is closed.

'Would you prefer ˌtea | or ˌcoffee?

c) in *wh* questions as a definite request for a piece of information

'Where is the ˌtoilet, ·please?

d) in imperative sentences

i) as a direct order or prohibition;

'Sit ˌdown. 'Don't ·smoke in ˌhere, ·please.

ii) as an instruction;

ˌPush to 'open the ˌdoor.

iii) as a strong form of offer.

'Have ·one of ˌmy ciga·rettes.

2 *High falling* ['] is used

a) in declarative sentences

i) in exclamations to indicate surprise, protest, enthusiasm, emphasis or insistence;

That's `excellent! You are `hurting me! 'Fancy `that!

ii) to indicate contrast with an element previously mentioned or believed to be in the listener's mind.

`No, | Mount `Elburz is the ·highest ·mountain in ·Europe.

b) in interrogative sentences, both those answerable by *yes* or *no* and *wh* questions

i) to insist on an answer being given;

'Did you `post ·that ·letter?

ii) to indicate surprise or irritation;
'Are you 'still ·not ·ready?

iii) in rhetorical questions of an exclamatory type, to which no answer is sought;
'Isn't she 'beautiful?

iv) in tag questions, to insist on the hearer's agreement to a proposition.
I 'told ·you | 'didn't I?

c) in imperative sentences

i) to insist on an order or prohibition where compliance is in doubt;
'Stop it, I ·say. 'Don't 'listen ·to him.

ii) to indicate the urgency of an instruction (e.g. because of imminent danger);
'Stop. 'Don't 'move.

iii) to insist on the acceptance of an offer.
'Do let me 'help you.

3   *Low rising* [,] is used

a) in declarative sentences

i) (with preceding low pitches) to indicate difference or resentment, guardedness, suspicion;
It ·doesn't ,matter. You ·shouldn't ·blame ,me.

ii) (with preceding high pitch) to reassure.
There's 'no ·need to be ,worried.

b) in interrogative questions, answerable by *yes* or *no*

i) to ask politely for confirmation or disconfirmation (also in tag questions);
You're 'French, ,aren't you?

ii) to make polite requests and offers;
'Would you ·please ·open the ,window? 'Can I do ·anything to ,help?

iii) in choice questions, to indicate that the list is open.
'Would you ·like ,tea | or ,coffee | or ·something ,stronger?

c) in *wh* questions

i) to indicate polite interest rather than a need for information;
'Where are you ·spending your ,holidays?

ii) to avoid the appearance of interrogation or peremptory questioning.
'What are you ,doing ·there?

d) in imperative sentences for gentle commands, especially to children, hospital patients, etc.
'Come and ·have your ·nice ˌbath. 'Just ·drink this ˌmedicine ·nicely.

4 *High rising* ['] is used

a) in declarative sentences (including isolated phrases and words used instead of full sentences)

i) to convert a statement into a question;
You were ·born in 'Scotland?

ii) to query what someone has said.
You ·say you're 'thirsty?

b) in interrogative questions answerable by *yes* or *no*

i) (with preceding low pitch) to indicate a casual enquiry;
(Would you) ·care for a 'sandwich?

ii) to repeat a question (with change of 1st and 2nd person) before answering.
A 'sandwich? Would I ·care for a 'sandwich?

c) in *wh* questions

i) to repeat a question (with change of 1st and 2nd person) before answering;
('Where do you ˌlive?) ·Where do I 'live?

ii) (with the *wh* word as nucleus) to ask for repetition of information given but not heard (or understood).
(He ·lives in (unintelligible)).
He ·lives 'where? 'Where does he ·live?

d) in imperative sentences to repeat an order, instruction or offer while deciding whether or how to comply
('Sit ˌdown, ·please.) ·Sit 'down? | 'Why ˌnot?

5 *Falling–rising* [ˇ] is used

a) in declarative sentences to convey various implications

i) warnings;
That ·jug is ˇhot!

ii) corrections;
Her ·dress 'is ˇgreen, you know. | It 'isn't ˇblue.

iii) demurral and limited agreement (with implied disagreement on the major issue);
I 'don't ·know if I a·gree with ˇthat.
ˇYes, | he 'is an ˇactive ·person.

    iv) mental reservations in making promises;
       ᵛYes, | I ᵛwill be ·good. || At ·least, I'll ᵛtry.

    v) uncertainty and hesitation;
       ·Yes ᵛpossibly. | I 'can't be ᵛcertain.

    vi) to soften the effect of bad news, conflict of views, etc.;
       You 'haven't ·done very ᵛwell, I'm a·fraid.
       You're ᵛwrong, you ·know.

    vii) (with attached tag questions) anxious query;
       You 'do ᵛlove me, ·don't you?

    viii) discouragement of a possible course of action;
       You can 'go to the ·cinema if you ᵛlike.

    ix) tentative advice;
       If 'I were ᵛyou ...

    x) implying that something has been left unsaid, which contrasts with, or contradicts what has been overtly stated;
       Your o·pinion is ᵛinteresting. (implying: but I 'don't a‚gree with it).

    xi) to query what has been said, implying that it is mistaken or untrue.
       'Seven ·eights are ·fifty ᵛfour?

b) in interrogative questions answered by *yes* or *no*

    i) to add a note of warning or doubt;
       Are you ᵛsure you ·locked the ·door?

    ii) when giving the answer to the question may be unwelcome to the person giving it.
       'Have you ·thought what might ·happen if you ᵛdid?

c) in *wh* questions

    i) to repeat a question, focusing on the key issue in contrast with other possible issues;
       'What did I ·do on ᵛFriday of ·last ·week?

    ii) (with the *wh* word as nucleus) to query a statement, implying scepticism regarding the element queried by the *wh* word employed.
       ᵛWhere did he ·find your ·purse?

d) in imperative sentences

    i) for issuing warnings rather than commands or instructions;
       'Watch where you're ᵛgoing. 'Don't ·try to ·pull the ᵛdoor ·open.

    ii) (with the imperative as nucleus) for pleading.
       ᵛDo ·try to be a ·little more ·careful.

Every tone group contains a *nucleus*. Many short utterances will comprise a single tone group, containing only one prominent syllable, which is then the nucleus of the tone group. Where there is more than one prominent syllable, the last of these is the nucleus and the first is the *head*. The head is usually marked by a jump up in pitch to a high-mid level. The actual pitch varies from mid to high, depending on the attitude of the speaker towards what he is saying and towards the hearer. The higher the level, the more cheerful and friendly the speaker sounds. The (high) head is marked in the texts by an upright line before the syllable concerned, above the line of writing [ˈ].

Non-prominent syllables, stressed or unstressed, which precede the head, are spoken on a low mid pitch. Those following a high head are kept on the same level, or form a descending sequence. Those following the nucleus conform to the configuration of the nucleus, as elaborated above. Stressed non-prominent syllables are marked in texts by a dot raised to mid-letter height [·]. As stated, they mark rhythmic beats in the utterance, but have no effect on the pitch pattern. Non-prominent unstressed syllables are left unmarked.

Many, perhaps most, short exchanges in conversation – especially the contributions of learners at *Threshold Level* – consist of single tone groups. Longer utterances may simply juxtapose tone groups as already described. However, compound (**and, but, either, or**) and complex (**if, because, when**) sentences may have two or more closely linked tone groups. Only in the last of these has the nucleus the functions listed above. The sequence is then termed a *major tone group*, and its completion is shown in a text with the mark [|||]. The constituent *minor tone groups* are marked [||]. The following are the most common types of sequence, and should be within the productive and receptive competence of *Threshold Level* learners:

1 Unemphatic, non-constructive sentences

non-final	final group
low rising	low falling
ˈWhen you ·see ˌJohn |	ˈtell him to ˌphone me.||

2 Contrasting

falling–rising	high falling
But ˈwhen you see ˇHarry |	ˈtell him I've ·left the ˋcountry.||

3 Main statement and modifier (non-contrastive)

low falling	low rising
I'm ˈleaving for ˋGermany |	on ˌFriday.||

4 Main statement and supplement

low fall	low fall
He ·lives in ˌLondon |	in a ˈsemi-de·tached ·house in ˌPeckham.||

5 In all cases of apposition, the same nuclear tone is used for both tone groups. the word **too** similarly repeats the tone of its antecedent nucleus.

'John ˌSmith, | a comˌputer ·programmer | ·lives in ˌCambridge, | a uniˌversity ·city.||
His 'brother ·lives there, | 'too.||

Note In this document, [|||] is omitted at the end of examples consisting of a single sentence.

Appendix B   Grammatical summary

This summary presents a classified inventory of the grammatical categories, elements and structures which figure as exponents of the functional and notional categories set out in Chapters 5–7.

Many critics of the original *Threshold Level* appear to have formed the impression that the functional and notional organisation adopted implied a neglect of grammar. We trust that a representation of grammatical content in a more systematic form than that originally adopted (which alphabetised the presentation for ease of reference) may correct that impression. In fact, the grammatical content is very rich and a learner who was able to exploit fully the resources required for the realisation of the range of functions and, particularly, general notions set out in Chapters 5 and 6 would have progressed well beyond what is to be expected from two years' part-time study. We therefore include some suggestions as to what use a learner can be expected to make of the grammatical resources, productively and receptively, in speech and writing, following the principles set out in the later chapters of the book. The symbol ® is employed in this chapter only to mark categories and exponents similarly marked in Chapter 5–7. It is not implied that all those unmarked are available for both receptive and productive use. Instead, users are recommended to follow the instructions made.

The order of presentation is ascending. That is to say that we first present grammatical information at the word level, classified according to the traditional parts of speech with which we expect most users to be familiar. Information is provided concerning the forms of words. Sub-classes are established in terms of the types and functions of words in the major classes set up. Phrases and clauses are then classified according to their formal structure and functional roles in the sentence. Finally, sentences are classified according to their structure and function. At all points cross-reference is made to the relevant sections of Chapters 5, 6 and 7. The same form of reference is used as that employed in the word index, i.e. first the chapter then the section and sub-sections into which the chapter is divided. So, for example, 6.3.2 refers to section 3.2 in Chapter 6. Examples are given, using only vocabulary which figures as exponents of the functional and notional categories presented in Chapters 5, 6 and 7 and collected together in the word index. The examples themselves give some idea of the range of expression made possible – far from the touristic minimalism some critics have deplored.

The summary is not conceived as a teaching or reference grammar of English, but as a guide to the resources to which a learner has access as a result of learning English to *Threshold Level*.

We trust that with a little experience users will find that the systematic presentation enables reference to be made quickly and efficiently as a further aid to curricular planning and course construction.

A   Word level

A 1   Nouns

1.1   Types of noun

1.1.1   proper nouns (written with an initial capital letter)

1.1.1.1 names of persons, towns and villages, brand names of products, etc.

These are not specified at *Threshold Level*, their relevance being a matter of personal experience. It is expected that a learner will be able to recognise or elicit and confirm the phonetic form of an unfamiliar proper name as well as to ask for and note down its spelling.

names of days (6.3.2), months (6.3.2, 7.1.4), cities (7.1.2), continents (7.1.2), countries (7.1.2), festivals (6.3.3), nationalities and languages (7.1.8), national currencies (7.9.6), political parties (7.6.5) and religions (7.1.12)

1.1.2   common nouns denoting uncountables

1.1.2.1 abstract, e.g. arts, sports and games (7.4.7), cardinal numbers (6.3.1, 6.4.1, 7.1.3), colours (6.5.1.9), points of the compass (6.2.1, 6.2.5)

1.1.2.2 nouns denoting materials, or mass substances, e.g. drinks (7.6.6, 7.10.1), foodstuffs (7.10.1), meals (7.3.1, 7.5.5, 7.10.1), means of transport (7.5.1, 7.5.2)

1.1.2.3 verbal nouns (gerund) e.g. heating (5.2.3), parking (5.5.3)

1.1.3   common nouns denoting countables: individuals, e.g. family members (7.1.11), job holders (7.1.10), animals (7.2.8), plants (7.2.8), objects such as clothes (7.9.3) and household articles (7.9.5), events such as accidents (7.7.4), measures (6.2.8.2, 4, 5)

1.2   Number (6.4.1)

1.2.1   regular written plural forms

1.2.1.1 -es added to singular form ending:

s	address, addresses
x	box, boxes
z	quiz, quizzes (note - zz-)
sh	brush, brushes
ch	match, matches
o	tomato, tomatoes
	(*but* piano, pianos)
	(following a consonant only),
y	lady, ladies (note i for y)

1.2.1.2 s added to singular form in other cases, including f(e) replaced by ve:
wife, wives
thief, thieves

1.2.2 regular spoken plural forms

1.2.2.1 /ɪz/ added to singular form ending:
/s/ /glɑːs/ /glɑːsɪz/ glass
/z/ /saɪz/ /saɪzɪz/ size
/ʃ/ /dɪʃ/ /dɪʃɪz/ dish
/ʒ/ /gæraːʒ/ /gæraːʒɪz/ garage
/tʃ/ /tʃɜːtʃ/ /tʃɜːtʃɪz/ church
/dʒ/ /dʒʌdʒ/ /dʒʌdʒɪz/ judge

1.2.2.2 /s/ added to singular form ending:
/p/ /stɒp/ /stɒps/ stop
/t/ /ædʌlt/ /ædʌlts/ adult
/k/ /bæk/ /bæks/ back
/f/ /lɑːf/ /lɑːfs/ laugh

1.2.2.3 /z/ added to singular form in other cases, including /θ,f/ replaced by /ð,v/:
/bɑːθ/ /bɑːðz/ bath
/naɪf/ /naɪvz/ knife

1.2.3 irregular plural forms

child, children	(7.1.11)
foot, feet	(7.7.1)
man, men	(7.1.6)
tooth, teeth	(7.7.1)
woman, women	(7.1.6)
penny, pence	(7.9.6)

1.2.4 The following nouns are found in the plural only:

clothes	(7.9.3)
means	(6.7.3.9)
people	(6.8.2)
scissors	(7.7.3)
tights	(7.9.3)
trousers	(7.9.3)

1.2.5 The following nouns are found in the singular only:

information	(7.5.1)
luggage	(7.5.6)
furniture	(7.2.3)
news	(7.4.3)

1.2.5.1 uncountable nouns (except in the sense of 'kinds of') (cf. A 1.1.2 above)

sugar	(7.10.1)
unemployment	(7.3.2)

1.3 Genitive

1.3.1 forms

1.3.1.1 spoken /z,s,ɪz/ (for use cf. A1.2.2 above) added to:

1.3.1.2 (written), 's:
all singular nouns
the man's head
plural nouns not ending in s
the children's room

1.3.1.3 '(written only; no affix in speech) added to plural nouns ending s
my aunts' house

1.3.2 Use

At *Threshold Level*, ability to use the genitive productively is required only with nouns denoting persons or animals. In other cases, *of* + NP may be used. The learners will be able to understand also such phrases as: a day's work, our country's Prime Minister.

Learners should be able to use the genitive to express the possessive relation (6.7.5.1), including ownership, but also other relationships such as parts of the body, kinship, social roles, mental and physical attributes and activities, etc.
Mary's feet, John's mother, the secretary's boss, the actor's performance, etc.

A 2   Pronouns

2.1   Types of pronoun

2.1.1   demonstrative (5.1.1, 6.8.1.1, 6.8.1.2)
this, that, these, those

2.1.2   personal (5.1.1, 6.8.1.1, 6.8.1.2)

2.1.2.1   subject forms
I, you, he, she, it, we, they

2.1.2.2   non-subject forms
me, you, him, her, it, us, them

2.1.3   possessive (6.8.1.1, 6.8.1.2)
mine, yours, his, hers, ours, theirs

2.1.4   relative (6.8.1.2)who, whom, which, that

2.1.5   interrogative (5.1.4, 6.8.1.1)
who, whom ❽, what, which, whose ❽

2.1.6   reflexive/emphatic (6.8.1.2)
myself, yourself, himself, herself, itself, ourselves, yourselves, themselves

2.1.7   prop word (6.8.1.2)
one

2.1.8   indefinite (6.8.2)
somebody, someone, something; anybody, anyone, anything; nobody, no-one, nothing; everybody, everyone, everything; some, all, any, none, each, both, it, you

2.2   Gender (3rd person singular only): masculine, feminine, neuter

2.2.1   forms
personal pronouns (subject)
he/she/it
(non-subject)
him/her/it
reflexive/emphatic
himself/herself/itself
possessive
his/hers

2.2.2   Use
At *Threshold Level*, learners should be able to use the pronouns he or she corresponding to the sex of the person or animal referred to, using it in other cases, e.g. for plants, things and abstracts. They should be aware of the traditional use of **he/him/himself/his** to refer anaphorically to a non-sex-specific personal noun and also of the alternative use of the plural forms, which are not gender-marked.
'Good ˌteachers | 'help their ·students to ·pass their examiˌnations **as against**
A 'good ˌteacher | 'helps his ·students to ·pass their examiˌnations.

A 3   Determiners

3.1   Definite article (5.1.1, 6.8.1.1)

3.1.1   forms
(written) **the**
(spoken) stressed /ðiː/
'She is the ˌwoman in my ·life.
unstressed before a consonant /ðə/
'Where's the ˌtoilet?
unstressed before a vowel /ði/
'What is the ·EˌU?

3.1.2   Use

3.1.2.1   with uniques
The ˌsun is ·shining.
(7.14.1)

3.1.2.2 with uniques for a given person or situation
'Send for the ˌdoctor. **(7.7.5)**

3.1.2.3 generically
The ˇcow | 'eats ˌgrass | and ·makes ˌmilk. **(7.2.8)**

3.1.2.4 anaphorically
'Italy is ˌbeautiful | and I 'like the ·country ·very ˌmuch.

3.1.2.5 when defined by an adjectival phrase or clause
the 'man over ˌthere
the 'woman I saw ˌyesterday

3.2 Indefinite article (6.8.2)

3.2.1 forms
(written)
before consonants a
before vowels an
(spoken)
stressed /eɪ/, /æn/
unstressed /ə/, /ən/

3.2.2 Use

3.2.2.1 for an unspecified person or thing (6.8.2)
There is a ˌman out·side.
'May I ·have an ˌorange?

3.2.2.2 to designate frequency (6.3.1.7)
·Take the ·medicine 'twice a ˌday.

3.2.2.3 to designate amount (6.4.2)
ˇApples | ·cost '35·p a ˌpound.

3.3 demonstrative (6.8.1.1, 6.8.1.2)
this, that, these those

3.4 possessive (6.7.5.1, 6.8.1.1, 6.8.1.2)
my, your, his, her, its, our, their

3.5 relative (6.8.1.2)
whose ®

3.6 interrogative (6.8.1.1)
which, whose ®

3.7 quantitative

3.7.1 indefinite (6.4.2)
some, any, no, every, much, many, more, most, several, few

3.7.2 distributive (6.8.2)
each

3.8 identifying (6.4.1)
another

3.9 pre-determiners all (6.4.2)
'All the ·guests have arˌrived.
such ® (6.4.3)
He is 'such a ˌstrange ·man.

3.10 post-determiners

3.10.1 cardinal numerals (6.4.1)
one, two, three, etc.

3.10.2 ordinal numbers (6.4.1)
first, second, third, etc.

3.10.3 identifying (6.7.4.1) other
The 'pain is in the ˎother ·leg.

····································

A 4 Adjectives

4.1 Participial

4.1.1 present, active Vinf + *ing*
a 'working ˌmother
'This ˌnovel | is ˌboring.

4.1.2 past, passive Vinf + *ed/en*
a 'closed ˌdoor
My 'pen is ˎbroken.

4.2 Attributive/predicative

4.2.1 attributive only
daily, weekly, main

4.2.2 predicative only
alive, all right, ill, well, so-so

4.2.3 other adjectives are used both attributively and predicatively

4.3 Gradable/non-gradable

4.3.1 non-gradable

4.3.1.1 numerals (6.4.1)

4.3.1.2 material (6.5.1.14)

4.3.1.3 categorial
married/single (7.1.7)
open/closed (6.5.1.12)

4.3.2   gradable

4.3.2.1 polar
old/young (6.5.1.10)
long/short (6.2.8.2)
large ⑧/small (6.2.8.1)
wide/narrow ⑧ (6.2.8.1)

4.3.2.2 neutralised polar
'How ˌold is your ·baby?

4.3.2.3 non-polar
colours (6.5.1.9)
taste (6.5.1.6)
smell (6.5.1.7)

4.4   **Comparison of gradable adjectives (6.4.3, 6.7.4.2)**

4.4.1   comparative of equality (6.7.4.1)

4.4.1.1 such
'Such ·men are ˌdangerous.

4.4.1.2 like
'This ·tastes like ˌcheese.

4.4.1.3 (the) same (as) (6.7.4.1)
'One ˌcar | is the 'same as aˌnother.

4.4.1.4 as + adj + as (6.7.4.2)
'That ˅stone | is as 'sharp as a ˌknife.

4.4.2   comparative of inequality
different (from) (6.7.4.1)
Malˈ˅tese | is ˋdifferent from Iˌtalian.
not so + adj + as ⑧ (6.7.4.2)
˅Wood | is 'not so 'heavy as ˌmetal.

4.4.3   comparative degree (6.7.4.2)
regular forms

4.4.3.1 (of monosyllabic adjectives)
adj+*er*
a 'longer ˌjourney

4.4.3.2 (of disyllabic adjectives with -*y*)
deleting -*y* and adding -*ier*
the ˌheavier ·suitcase

4.4.3.3 (of some other disyllabics)
adj+*er*
'a 'quieter ˌroom

4.4.3.4 (of other polysyllabic adjectives) *more* + adj
a ·more 'comfortable ˌchair

4.4.3.5 (of negative adjectives with *un-*)
more + *un-*+adj alternatively
a ·more un'pleasant occuˌpation
less + positive adj
a 'less ˌpleasant occu·pation

4.4.4   superlative degree (6.7.4.2)
regular forms

4.4.4.1 (of monosyllabic adjectives)
adj+*est*
the 'oldest ·man aˌlive

4.4.4.2 (of disyllabic adjectives with -*y*)
deleting -*y* and adding -*iest*
the 'earliest ˌtrain

4.4.4.3 (of some other disyllabics)
adj+*est*
the 'bitterest ˌpill

4.4.4.4 (of other polysyllabic adjectives)
most + adj
the 'most 'useful ˌdictionary

4.4.5   irregular comparatives
good, better, best, bad, worse, worst

4.5   **Complementising adjectives (i.e. adjectives regularly taking particular complementation structures. See C2.1.1.4 below.)**

4.5.1   of probability (5.2.9–10)
possible, probable

4.5.2   of certainty (5.2.13–14)
certain, sure

4.5.3   of evaluation (6.5.2)
good, bad, wrong

4.5.4   denoting emotional states
(5.2.29–50)
happy, glad, sorry

4.5.5   denoting moral obligations
(5.2.19)
allowed, permitted, free

4.5.6   denoting physical qualities
(6.5.1)
hard, hot, dry

4.5.7   denoting moral qualities
(5.2.49, 5.3.3)
kind, nice, good

4.5.8   denoting order (6.3.9)
first, second, next, last

A 5   Adverbs

5.1   **Functions of adverbs**

5.1.1   existential (6.1.1)
There is a ˌman at the ·door.

5.1.2   of time (6.3)
always, already, now, then, ago

5.1.3   place (6.2)
here, there

5.1.4   manner (6.7.3.9)
fast, hard, well

5.1.5   degree (6.4.3)
very, quite, too

5.1.6   direction (6.2.5)
up, down, away

5.1.7   arrangement (6.2.7)
first, last

5.1.8   anteriority (6.3.7)
before, already, yet

5.1.9   posteriority (6.3.8)
afterwards

5.1.10   sequence (6.3.9)
then, next, first, secondly, lastly

5.1.11   simultaneity (6.3.10)
at the same time

5.1.12   future reference (6.3.11)
soon, tomorrow

5.1.13   present reference (6.3.12)
now, still

5.1.14   past reference (6.3.13)
just, recently

5.1.15   frequency (6.3.17)
always, often, sometimes

5.1.16   intermittence (6.3.19)
sometimes

5.1.17   permanence (6.3.20)
always

5.1.18   repetitiousness (6.3.22)
again

5.1.19   uniqueness (6.3.23)
(only) once

5.1.20   change (6.3.27)
suddenly

5.1.21   preferences (5.2.27)
rather ... than

5.2   **Form**

5.2.1   simple
fast, hard, now, **etc.**

5.2.2   adj+*ly*
quickly, certainly, etc.

5.3   **Types of adverb**

5.3.1   indefinite (6.8.2)
**anywhere, everywhere,
somewhere, nowhere, always,
never, sometimes**

5.3.2   deictic (6.8.1.1) (and
anaphoric (6.8.1.2))
here, there, now, then

5.3.3 interrogative (6.8.1.1)
relative (6.8.1.2)

5.3.3.1 time
when (?)
'When will he ˏcome?
I ˎheard him ·when he ·left.

5.3.3.2 place
where (?)
'Where is my ˏpen?
'This | is ·where it ˏis.

5.3.3.3 manner
how (?)
'How do you ˏknow?
I ˎknow | ·how to ˏdo it.

5.3.3.4 reason
why (?)
'Why did he ˏgo?
I ˎknow | ·why he ˏwent.

5.4 **Comparison of gradable adverbs**

5.4.1 monosyllabic
fast

5.4.1.1 comparative: adv+*er*
faster

5.4.1.2 superlative: adv+*est*
fastest

5.4.2 polysyllabic (adj+*ly*)
gladly

5.4.2.1 comparative: *more* + adv
more gladly

5.4.2.2 superlative: *most* + adv
most gladly.
but early, earlier, earliest
(not adj+*ly*)

5.4.3 irregular comparatives
well, better, best;
badly, worse, worst;
far, further, furthest;
little, less, least

A 6   Preposition

6.1   **Types**

6.1.1 of position (6.2.2)
above Ⓡ, against, among Ⓡ at,
before Ⓡ, behind, below Ⓡ,
between, in, inside Ⓡ, on,
opposite, outside, over, round,
under, with

6.1.2 distance (6.2.3)
near

6.1.3 direction (6.2.5)
across Ⓡ, along, down Ⓡ, for,
from, into, off, past, through,
to, towards Ⓡ, up Ⓡ

6.1.4 origin (6.2.6)
from,

6.1.5 arrangement (6.2.7)
after, before, between, among

6.1.6 time (6.3)

6.1.6.1 point of time (6.3.3)
at, by, in, on

6.1.6.2 duration (6.3.4)
during, for, from ... to,
since, till, until Ⓡ

6.1.6.3 anteriority (6.3.7)
before

6.1.6.4 posteriority (6.3.8)
after

6.1.6.5 future reference (6.3.11)
in

6.1.6.6 frequency (6.3.17)
on

6.1.7 manner (6.7.3.9)
as, by, with

6.1.8 agency (6.7.3.1)
by

6.1.9 instrumentality (6.7.3.4)
with, through

6.1.10 benefaction (6.7.3.5)
for

6.1.11 possession (6.7.5.1)
of, with

6.1.12 inclusion/exclusion (6.7.6.3)
with/without

6.1.13 similarity (6.7.4.2)
as ... as, like

6.2   Use
At *Threshold Level*, learners
should understand and
produce the above prepositions
in the functions given, together
with the phrasal prepositions
listed in B6 below, as exponents
of the functional and notional
categories set out in Chapters 5,
6 and 7. They cannot be
expected to extrapolate from
those to other, often arbitrary,
uses of prepositions in
adverbial phrases and phrasal
verbs.

A 7   Verbs

7.1   Types of verb

7.1.1   intransitive verbs, denoting:

7.1.1.1 actions
dance, play (7.4.4)
talk (7.6.2)

7.1.1.2 motion (6.2.4)
come, go, fall, leave, move
follow

7.1.1.3 existence (6.1.1)
be, exist, happen (5.1.4.3, 6.1.4)

7.1.1.4 weather conditions (7.14.1)
rain, snow

7.1.2   transitive (passim)
bring, take, carry, kill
pull, push, put

7.1.3   causative (6.7.3.6)
have, get, make

7.1.4   inchoative (6.3.27)
become, get, go, turn
fall, start (5.5.3.5, 6.2.4)

7.1.5   resultative
win, lose (7.4.7)
qualify, pass (7.3.5)
succeed

7.1.6. factitive
make (6.1.1, 6.5.1.14, 7.3.1,
7.4.6)
cook (7.3.1)

7.1.7   complementising verbs (i.e.
verbs with clausal
complementation. See
B 6.5.1.4 and C 2.1.1.5 below.)
denoting:

7.1.7.1 cognitive attitudes (5.2)
think, believe, know
forget, remember, wonder

7.1.7.2 volition (5.2.23–27)
like, want, intend, prefer

7.1.7.3 emotions (5.2.29–44)
love, hate, enjoy, care,
surprise, expect, hope

7.1.7.4 commencement (6.3.24)
begin, start

7.1.7.5 cessation (6.3.25)
end, stop, finish

7.1.7.6 sensory perception (6.5.1.4–7)
watch, hear, see, taste, smell,
look

7.1.7.7 suasion (6.6.2)
order, tell, request,
recommend, invite, forbid, ask,
teach

7.1.7.8 reflection (6.6.1)
think, believe, hope, know

7.1.7.9 expression (6.6.2)
say, answer, ask, tell

7.1.7.10 appearance (5.2.13)
seem

7.2   Simple forms: regular

7.2.1 infinitive: (*to* +) verb stem
(to) accept, agree, live, try

7.2.2 participles:

7.2.2.1 present: verb stem (less -e
after consonant) + *ing*
accepting, agreeing, living, trying

7.2.2.2 past

7.2.2.2.1 (written)
verb stem +*(e)d*
(replacing y by i after
consonant)
accepted, agreed, lived, tried

7.2.2.2.2 (spoken)
verb stem + /ɪd/
after /t, d/
accepted, ended
verb stem + /t/ after /p, k, f, s, ʃ,
tʃ/
hoped, asked, laughed, crossed,
danced, mixed, pushed, watched
verb stem + /d/ after all other
consonants and all vowels

7.2.3 gerund: as present participle

7.2.4 finite

7.2.4.1 present (6.3.11, 12, 14)
I/you/we/they accept, agree,
live, try
verb stem (+ *(e)s* in 3rd person
singular)
he/she/it accepts, agrees, lives,
tries

7.2.4.2 past: as past participle

7.3   Simple forms: irregular

7.3.1 be
non-finite a) simple infinitive
be
b) present participle
being

c) past participle
been
d) gerund
being
finite a) unmarked (present)
I am,
you/we/they are,
he/she/it is
b) past
I/he/she/it was
you/we/they were

7.3.2 have
non-finite a) simple infinitive
have
b) present participle
having
c) past participle
had
d) gerund
having
finite a) present
I/you/we/they have/'ve
he/she/it has/'s
b) past
had/'d

7.3.3 do
non-finite a) simple infinitive
do
b) present participle
doing
c) past participle
done
d) gerund
doing
finite a) present
I/you/we/they do,
he/she/it does
b) past
did

7.3.4 Modal auxiliary verbs
These have no non-finite
forms, but only unmarked
(present) and past finite
forms, positive and negative:

can	can't	could	couldn't
may	mayn't	might	mightn't
must	mustn't	must	mustn't
shall	shan't	should	shouldn't
will/'ll	won't	would/'d	wouldn't

7.3.5 Other irregular verbs differ from regular verbs only in
 a) the past finite and
 b) the past participle.
The a) infinitive, b) past finite and c) past participle forms for irregular verbs which figure as exponents in the *Threshold Level* specifications are:

become	became	become
begin	began	begun
break	broke	broken
bring	brought	brought
buy	bought	bought
choose	chose	chosen
come	came	come
cost	cost	cost
cut	cut	cut
do	did	done
draw	drew	drawn
drive	drove	driven
drink	drank	drunk
eat	ate	eaten
fall	fell	fallen
feel	felt	felt
fight	fought	fought
find	found	found
fly	flew	flown
forbid	forbade	forbidden
forget	forgot	forgotten
forgive	forgave	forgiven
freeze	froze	frozen
get	got	got
give	gave	given
go	went	gone
have	had	had
hold	held	held
hurt	hurt	hurt
keep	kept	kept
know	knew	known
leave	left	left
let	let	let
lie	lay	lain
lose	lost	lost
make	made	made
mean	meant	meant
meet	met	met
pay	paid	paid
put	put	put
ride	rode	ridden
say	said	said
see	saw	seen
sell	sold	sold
send	sent	sent
shine	shone	shone
shoot	shot	shot
show	showed	shown
shut	shut	shut
sing	sang	sung
sleep	slept	slept
speak	spoke	spoken
spend	spent	spent
stand	stood	stood
steal	stole	stolen
strike	struck	struck
swim	swam	swum
take	took	taken
teach	taught	taught
tell	told	told
think	thought	thought
throw	threw	thrown
understand	understood	understood
undo	undid	undone
wear	wore	worn
win	won	won
write	wrote	written

7.4 Compound forms (regular and irregular)

7.4.1 forms

7.4.1.1 perfective
 have + past participle

7.4.1.2 progressive (continuous)
 be + present participle

7.4.1.3 passive
 be + past participle

7.4.1.4 modal auxiliary + infinitive

7.4.2 Use
Of the many combinations which are possible, learners at *Threshold Level* should be able to use productively:

7.4.2.1 modal + simple infinitive (5.2.15–20; 5.2.22; 5.3; 6.3.11)
The ·train will ar·rive at '10 p.‚m.

7.4.2.2 present continuous (6.3.12, 21)
'Are you ‚listening to me?

7.4.2.3 past continuous (6.3.13, 18)
The 'car was ‚waiting for us | when we ar'rived.

7.4.2.4 present perfect (6.3.7, 12, 18)
We have 'often been | to ‚Paris.

7.4.2.5 past perfect (6.3.7)
I had 'never ·seen her be‚fore.

7.4.3 Learners should also be aware of other combinations and understand their gist.
I've been ·waiting for a 'long ‚time.
'If I had ‚known, | I would have ‚told you.

7.5 **Uses of be, have, and do**

7.5.1 be

7.5.1.1 (as copula) + predicative adjective
'John is ‚tired.

7.5.1.2 (as copula) + noun phrase (5.1.1.4)
'Mary is a ‚hospital ·worker.

7.5.1.3 (as copula) + prepositional phrase (6.2.1)
ˇCornwall | is in the 'West of ‚England.

7.5.1.4 (as copula) + adverb
Our ‚guests are ·here.

7.5.1.5 existential (6.1)
There are '30 ‚cows on the ·farm.

7.5.1.6 (+ from) origin (7.1.9)
She is from 'New ‚Zealand.

7.5.1.7 age (6.5.1.10)
He is ‚six.

7.5.1.8 point of time (6.3.3)
It is '6 p.‚m.

7.5.1.9 to act as a part (7.4.4)
'Judi ˇDench | is 'Lady Mac‚beth.

7.5.1.10 (perfective aspect + *to*) to visit (6.2.1)
She has 'never ·been to ‚London.

7.5.1.11 to cost (6.5.2.1)
'How ·much are ·those ‚trousers?

7.5.1.12 (as auxiliary) + present participle (continuous aspect) (6.3.12, 13)
She is 'reading a ‚book.

7.5.1.13 (as auxiliary) + past participle (passive voice) cf. A 7.7.9 below (5.3.7, 6.7.3)
'England were de·feated by Aus‚tralia.

7.5.2 have

7.5.2.1 possession i.e. ownership or the right to use the objects, accommodation, transport, services, etc. (6.7.5.1)
They ·have a 'house in the ‚country.

7.5.2.2 attribution, e.g. name (5.5.2)
He has a ·name | 'can't pro‚nounce.
address (7.1.2)
They have an ad'dress in ‚Mayfair.
telephone number (7.1.3)
We have a 'new ‚telephone ·number.

family (7.1.11)
She has 'four ˌchildren | and 'six ˌgrandchildren.
friends (7.6.1)
We have 'friends in ˌStrasbourg.
occupation (7.1.10)
salary (7.3.3)
She has a 'new ˌjob | and a 'better ˌsalary.
accommodation (7.2.1, 2)
We have a 'flat in ˌIslington.
pets (7.2.8)
Our ·daughter has a 'cat and a ˌdog.
hobbies (7.4.2)
My ·husband has an un'usual ˌhobby.
bank account (7.11.4), etc.
They ·say he has a 'bank ac·count in ˌSwitzerland.
qualifications (7.8.3)
My 'son has a de·gree in ecoˌnomics.

7.5.2.3 characteristics, e.g. size (6.2.8), shape (6.5.1.1), taste (6.5.1.6), smell (6.5.1.7), colour (6.5.1.9)
ᵛLeaves | have 'many ·different ˌcolours, | ˌshapes | and ˌsizes.

7.5.2.4 part–whole relations,
The ·plane has 'four ˌengines.
membership of clubs, parties, etc.
Our ·club has '2,·000 ˌmembers.

7.5.2.5 to get, receive, e.g. guests (7.5.5), a letter (7.6.3)
We have ˌguests | this ˌweekend.

7.5.2.6 to take part in, experience or undergo a process or event, e.g. meals (7.3.1)
We had a 'good ˌmeal | ·last ˌnight.
(7.10.1, 2), toiletry (7.7.3)
You 'must have a ˌbath | or a 'good ˌwash.

leisure activities, hobbies (7.4)
We are ·having a ˋparty | toˌnight. ˋDo ˌcome!
holidays, travel (7.5)
'Have a ·good ·journey ˌhome!
ailments (7.7.4)
She has a 'bad ˌcold.
operation (7.7.4)
'When is she ·having her operˌation?
appointments (7.7.5)
'Have you an apˌpointment with the ·doctor?
education (7.8)
She 'had her eduˌcation | in ˌFrance.
weather (7.14)
We had a ˋthunderstorm | last ˌnight.

7.5.2.7 (+ *to*) obligation (5.2.15)
I 'have to ˌgo ·now.

7.5.2.8 (+ past participle) (perfective aspect) (6.3.7)
They have 'gone aˌway.

7.5.2.9 (+ NP + infinitive VP) causative
'Why not have the ˌgarage ·clean your ·car?

7.5.2.10 (+ NP + past participle) (causative) (5.3.3.7, 6.7.3.6)
I 'have my ·shirts ·made in ·Hong ˌKong.

7.5.3 do

7.5.3.1 perform an action
I 'always ·do the ·washing-ˌup.

7.5.3.2 pro-verb (6.8.1.2)
I am sup'posed to ˌrest | and I ˌdo.
('Can I have an ˌapple?) 'Please ˌdo.

7.5.3.3 intensifying (5.1.3)
I ˋdo ·like a ·good ˌwine!

7.5.3.4 correction (5.1.3)
But I ˋdid ·tell you!

7.5.3.5 negation (5.2.1, 2, 4, etc.)
It 'doesn't ˌrain | in the ˌdesert.

7.5.3.6 interrogative (5.1.4)
'Do you ·eat ˌcheese?

7.5.3.7 tag questions
You ·work in an 'office, | ˌdon't you?

7.5.3.8 tag responses (5.2.1, 2)
ˌYes, | I ˌdo. ˌNo, | I ˌdon't.

7.5.3.9 in special interrogative
'Where do you ˌlive?

7.5.3.10 strong imperatives and invitations (5.3.10)
`Do ·sit ˌdown!

7.6   Uses of modal auxiliaries

7.6.1   can

7.6.1.1 ability, capacity (5.2.17, 18) (6.5.2.10)
This ·actress can ·sing 'very ˌwell.

7.6.1.2 requests (5.3.3, 8, 14)
'Can you ·do ˌthis ·for me?

7.6.1.3 offers (5.3.9)
'Can I ˌhelp you?

7.6.1.4 permission (5.2.19, 20, 22)
'Can I ˌgo now?

7.6.1.5 possibility (5.2.9, 10)
It `cannot ·snow | in ˅Ghana.

7.6.1.6 sensory experience (6.5.1.4, 5)
I can ·see some `animals.

7.6.2   could

7.6.2.1 past of can (6.3.13)
Mithri˅dates | could ·speak 'many ˌlanguages.
indirect speech (5.6.13.5) ®
I ·said that you could 'come ˌin.

7.6.2.2 tentative offers ®
'Could I be of ·any ˌhelp?

7.6.2.3 tentative requests
'Could you ·speak more ˌslowly, ·please?

7.6.2.4 suggesting a course of action (5.3.1)
We could ·go to the `cinema.

7.6.2.5 suggestions ®
You could 'always ask a po˅liceman the ·way.

7.6.2.6 hypothetical possibility ®
You could 'easily get `lost | if you ·went on ˌfoot.

7.6.3   may

7.6.3.1 possibility (5.2.9, 10)
It 'may `rain | this afterˌnoon.

7.6.3.2 asking permission (5.2.19, 20)
'May I ·drive the ˌcar?
including also:
making introductions
'May I intro·duce my ˌhusband?
wants and desires (5.2.23)
'May I ·watch ˌtelevision?
asking someone for something (5.3.14)
'May I ·have a ˌsweet?
interrupting (5.5.14)
'May ˌI ·say ·something?

7.6.4   might

7.6.4.1 suggesting a course of action (5.3.1)
We 'might per·haps ·go to `France.

7.6.5   must

7.6.5.1 logical necessity (5.2.9, 10, 11, 12)
He ·speaks 'Flemish and ˌFrench. ||
He ·must be `Belgian.

7.6.5.2 physical necessity (5.2.11)
We must ˌall ·die | 'sooner or ˌlater.

7.6.5.3 obligation/compulsion (5.2.15, 16)
You must ·eat 'everything on your ˌplate.

7.6.5.4 prohibition (5.2.19)
You must 'not ·smoke in ˏhere.

7.6.5.5 pressing invitations (5.3.10)
You 'must ·come and ˏstay with us.

7.6.5.6 emphatic statements (5.5.8)
I 'must ·stress the ·fact that our ·currency is ˏweak.

7.6.6 shall

7.6.6.1 future tense (1st person)
I/We shall be in `London | ·next ˏweek.

7.6.6.2 making an offer
'Shall I ·cook the ˏmeal?

7.6.6.3 suggesting a course of action (5.3.1)
'Shall we ·go to the ˏtheatre?

7.6.7 should

7.6.7.1 past of shall (6.3.13)
He 'said it should be ˏdone.

7.6.7.2 advice (5.3.4)
You should be ˏcareful.

7.6.7.3 duty (6.5.2.3)
You should 'do your ˏbest.

7.6.7.4 expectation
The 'train should be `there | by ˏnow.

7.6.7.5 rightness, wrongness (6.5.2.3)
We should 'help our ˏmothers.

7.6.8 will ('ll)

7.6.8.1 future reference (6.3.11)
The ·sun will ·rise at '6 a.ˏm. toˏmorrow.

7.6.8.2 expressing/enquiring about certainty (5.2.9)
It will ˏrain | this afterˏnoon.

7.6.8.3 promises (5.2.25)
I will 'pay you ·next ˏweek.

7.6.8.4 requests (5.3.3)
'Will you ·sit ˏdown, ·please.

7.6.8.5 asking if an invitation is accepted or not (5.3.13)
'Will you ʼvisit us, ·after ·all?

7.6.8.6 invitations
'Will you ·come to ˏdinner with us?

7.6.8.7 expressing dissatisfaction/dissatisfaction (5.2.35, 36)
'That will ('not) ˏdo.

7.6.8.8 prediction
Toˇmorrow | will be 'warm and ˏsunny.

7.6.8.9 intentions
I will go to `London | ·next ˏweek.

7.6.8.10 (im)possibility (5.2.9, 10)
The ˏcar ·won't ·start.

7.6.8.11 capacity (6.5.2.10)
Our ·car will 'only ·run on ˏleaded ·petrol.

7.6.9 would

7.6.9.1 past of will (6.3.13)
The ˏcar ·wouldn't ·start.

7.6.9.2 indirect speech ®
He 'thought he would ·go to `London | the ·next ˏday.

7.6.9.3 enquiring about wants/desires (5.2.24)
'Would you ·like an ·iceˏcream?

7.6.9.4 invitations (5.3.10)
'Would you ·like to ·come to ·us for a ˏmeal?

7.6.9.5 polite requests (5.3.3)
'Would you ·close the ˏwindow, ·please?

7.6.9.6 hypothetical conditions (6.7.6.8)
If you ˇasked me, | I would `come.

7.6.9.7 unreal conditions (6.7.6.8) ®
If you had ˅asked me, | I would have ˎcome.

7.6.9.8 advice (5.3.4)
If ˅I were ·you, | I'd ·go by ˎtrain.

7.6.9.9 preference (5.2.27, 28)
I'd 'rather ·drink ˎcoffee | than ˎtea.

7.7   Use of verb forms

7.7.1   simple present

7.7.1.1 general statement without time reference (6.3.14)
'Cats and ˎdogs | are ˎanimals.

7.7.1.2 permanently ongoing present actions (6.3.12)
My 'sister ·works in a ˎfactory.

7.7.1.3 habitual actions (6.3.17, 22)
I ·go to ·bed at '11 p.ˎm. | 'every ˎnight.

7.7.1.4 future reference with adverbs etc. denoting future time (6.3.11)
The ·train ˎleaves | ˎsoon.

7.7.1.5 present reference with verbs (cf. A 7.2.4.1 above) denoting:
cognitive attitudes (5.2)
I ·think she is ˎFrench.
volition (5.2.23–27)
He 'wants to ·go to ˎbed.
emotions (5.2.29–44)
I 'hope the ·plane will ·leave on ˅time.
sensory perception (6.5.1.4–7)
·This ·food tastes ˎgood.
reflection (6.6.1)
I 'know you are ˎtired.
appearance (5.2.13)
He ·seems to be aˎsleep.

7.7.2   simple past forms

7.7.2.1 verbs denoting actions completed in a past period (6.3.13)
I ·saw 'Helen | ˎyesterday.

7.7.2.2 reporting statements and questions which contained simple present verb forms (5.6.13)
He ·said 'dogs and ˎcats | were ˎanimals.
He 'asked if my ·sister ·worked in a ˎfactory.

7.7.2.3 for the equivalents of simple present usage (cf. A 7.7.1 above) but relating to a past period (6.3.13):
general statements
˅Formerly, | there were '240 ·pence to ˎ£1.
permanent states
As a ˅child, | I ·lived in ˎLondon.
habitual actions
'Last ˎyear, | I ˎdrove to ·work every ·day.
stative verbs (cf. A 7.7.1.5 above)
He 'thought it was ·time to ˎgo.

7.7.3   present perfect (with reference to the present time)

7.7.3.1 anteriority (6.3.7)
'Have you seen ˎMary?

7.7.3.2 past reference (6.3.13) i.e. a past action seen as leading to a present condition
It has 'stopped ˎraining.
(implying: It is not now raining.)

7.7.3.3 continuity (6.3.18) i.e. an action or state, beginning in the past, which is still continuing
I have ·known ·Peter for 'ten ˎyears, | since I 'met him in ˎMunich.

7.7.4   past perfect (with the same) denotations as the present perfect, but with reference to a previous time)

7.7.4.1 anteriority (6.3.7)
He had 'met ˏMary | ·earlier that ˏday.

7.7.4.2 past reference (6.3.13)
The 'guests had arˏrived.

7.7.4.3 continuity (6.3.18)
In 19ᵛ80, | when he ᵛdied, | I had ·known ·Peter for 'ten ˏyears.

7.7.4.4 in indirect speech (5.6.13), reporting past statements and questions containing present perfect forms
He 'asked if she had ·seen ˏMary ·lately.
She ·said the 'guests had arˏrived.

7.7.5 present continuous

7.7.5.1 future reference with verbs of motion (6.3.11)
We are ·driving to ˋScotland ·next ˏweek.

7.7.5.2 proximal future (6.3.11)
be + going to + infinitive
I am ·going to ·sit here 'all ˏday.

7.7.5.3 for present reference i.e. for an action in progress at the time of speaking
Our 'son is ·sitting ·quietly ·watching ˏtelevision.

7.7.5.4 continuity (6.3.18)
It is 'still ˏraining.

7.7.5.5 temporariness (6.3.21) especially with stative verbs (cf. A 7.7.1.5 above)
I am in'tending to go to ˏFrance for ·Easter. (implying 'but I may change my mind')

7.7.6 past continuous (used with the same denotations as the present continuous, when the frame of reference is the past (6.3.13))

7.7.6.1 future motion (6.3.11)
He was ·driving to ˏScotland the ·next ˏday.

7.7.6.2 proximal future reference
be + going to + infinitive
He was going to ·wait a 'long ˏtime.

7.7.6.3 action in progress (6.3.18)
She was 'writing a ˏletter | when the ˏtelephone ·rang.

7.7.6.5 continuity (6.3.18)
He was 'still ·studying to ·be a ˏlawyer

7.7.6.5 temporariness (6.3.21)
The 'students were ·working as ˏwaiters.

7.7.6.6 in indirect speech (5.6.13), reporting past statements and questions containing present continuous forms. ®
He .said it was 'still ˏraining.

The following uses are for receptive use only by learners at *Threshold Level*:

7.7.7 present perfect continuous ®

7.7.7.1 continuity (6.3.18) in a present frame of reference ®
I have been ·standing here since 'six o'ˏclock.

7.7.8 past perfect continuous ®

7.7.8.1 continuity (6.3.18) in a past frame of reference ®
He had been ·learning ·French for 'ten ˏyears | and 'spoke it ˏwell.

7.7.8.2 in indirect speech (6.3.18), reporting statements and questions containing verbs in the past continuous or present perfect continuous ®
He ·said he had been ·playing ˏtennis (reporting either 'I have been playing tennis', or 'I was playing tennis').

7.7.9 passive voice (5.3.7.3)

7.7.9.1 forms (cf. A 7.4.1.3 and
A 7.5.1.13 above):
passive with by adjunct ®
He was 'warned by the po,lice.
agentless passive
My ,purse has been ·stolen.

7.7.9.2 role of subject
corresponding to the direct
object in an active sentence
(6.7.3.2) ®
The 'train was de·layed by ,fog.
**corresponding to the indirect
object in an active sentence
(6.7.3.3)** ®
I was ·given a'nother ,room |
when I ,asked for it.

7.7.9.3 Use
At *Threshold Level* learners
should be able to understand
passive sentences, e.g. in
instructions (5.3.7). Productive
ability will be confined to the
use of the agentless passive
where the subject of the
corresponding active sentence
is unknown or irrelevant and
particularly with the following
verbs:
to be allowed (5.2.19)
ᵛSmoking | is 'not al,lowed.
permitted (5.2.19)
'Smoking is per,mitted.
**baked, boiled, fried, grilled
(7.10.1)**
I pre'fer my ·fish to be ,grilled.
included (7.10.2)
'Service is in·cluded in the ,bill.
seen (6.5.1.4), heard (6.5.1.5)
ᵛChildren | should be 'seen and
·not ,heard.
called (7.1.1)
The ˋpub in our ,village | is ·called
'The 'King's ,Head'.
operated (up)on (7.7.4)
He was 'operated (up)on for
'cancer of the ,stomach.

trained (7.8.1)
He was 'trained as an elec·tronic
engi,neer.

A 8   Conjunctions

8.1 **Co-ordinating (joining
constituents of equal rank.
See C 1 and D 1 below.)**

8.1.1 conjunctive (6.7.6.1)

8.1.1.1 and
**joining non-contrastive
constituents of the same rank**
She is 'always ,happy | and
,beautiful | and 'she and ·I are in
,love | and in'tend to get
,married.
**expressing sequence of
actions**
He 'went to the ,station | and
'took the ·train to ,London.

8.1.1.2 but
**joining contrastive
constituents**
He is inᵛtelligent | but ,lazy.

8.1.1.3 as well as ®
He is in'telligent | as 'well as
,active.

8.1.1.4 ... as + adjective/verb + as ...
He is as 'strong as a ,horse.
He ·works as 'hard as he ,can.

8.1.2 disjunctive (6.7.6.2)

8.1.2.1 or (inclusive)
·This ·play is 'good for ,children |
or ,older ·people.

8.1.2.2 or (exclusive)
'Are you ,married | or ,single?

8.2 **Subordinating (cf. C 2 below)**

8.2.1 complementising **that**
I 'hope that he will ,come.

8.2.2 temporal (6.3): after (6.3.8), before (6.3.7), since, until (6.3.4), when (6.3.3), while (6.3.10)
He 'left before I ar‚rived.

8.2.3 spatial (6.2); where (6.2.1), preposition + which
The 'town where/in which I ‚live | is in ‚Dorset.

8.2.4 manner (6.7.3.9): how, how + adverb
'Teach me ·how you ·make an ‚omelette.
I 'know how ·hard you ‚work.

8.2.5 reason, cause (6.7.6.4, 6): as ⓡ, because, since ⓡ
We are ‚glad | be·cause the ‚sun is ·shining.

8.2.6 effect, consequence (6.7.6.5) so (+ adj + that)
It was 'so ‚hot | that I 'took off my ‚coat. or It was ‚hot, | so I 'took off my ‚coat.

8.2.7 conditional (6.7.6.8)
If it 'doesn't ‚rain, | we'll ·go ‚fishing.

8.2.8 relative (6.8.1.1, 2): what, who, whom, that, which, whose
'What you ·say ‚interests me.
I ‚know | ·who you ‚mean.

B Phrase level

B 1 Noun phrase (NP)

1.1 Form

1.1.1 a pronoun
She ‚loves him.

1.1.2 a noun without determiner

1.1.2.1 proper nouns
'Juan ·lives in ‚Spain.

1.1.2.2 plural indefinites (cf. A 1.2 above)
'People are ‚strange.

1.1.2.3 unspecified singular nouns denoting:
colour (6.5.1.9)
'red, ·white and ‚blue
material (6.5.1.14)
I pre·fer 'leather·shoes.
days, months (6.3.2, 6.3.3)
To·morrow is 'Tuesday the ·fourth of ‚April.
drinks (7.10.1)
'Beer tastes ‚bitter.
foodstuffs (7.10.1)
I 'don't 'eat | ‚meat.
meals (7.3.1, 7.10.1)
'What is for ‚lunch to·day?
festivals (6.3.3)
'Easter is ‚early | ·this ‚year.
numerals (6.4.1)
'Three and ‚eight | make e‚leven.
abstracts (7.8)
Edu'cation is im‚portant.
arts, sports, games (7.4.2)
I pre·fer 'music | or 'chess | to ‚football.
vehicles seen as means of transport (7.5.1)
I 'go to ‚London | by 'car or by ‚train.

1.1.13 determiner + noun (cf. A 3 above)
'Put a ‚stamp on ·this ·envelope.

1.1.4 pre-determiner (cf. A 3.9 above) + determiner + noun
'Did she ·eat ·all the ‚cakes?

1.1.5 (pre-determiner) + determiner + post determiner (cf. A 3.10 above) + noun
Is 'this your ·first ‚visit to ·Britain?

1.1.6 (pre-determiner +) (determiner +) (post-determiner +) adjective(s) + noun
She was ·wearing a 'nice ·new ·white ‚dress.

1.1.7 (determiner +) adverb of degree (6.4.3) + adjective + noun
ᵛChess is a 'very ˏdifferent ˙game.

1.1.8 (determiner +) qualifying adverb + adjective + noun
He is a 'happily ˙married ˏman.

1.1.9 (determiner +) (adverb +) (adjective +) noun + relative adjunct:

1.1.9.1 adverb
'Do you ˙know the ˙way ˏback?

1.1.9.2 prepositional phrase
The 'chair in the ˏbedroom | is ˏbroken.

1.1.9.3 to + infinitive verb phrase (VPinf)
I ˙need a 'clean ˏshirt to ˙wear.

1.1.10 (determiner +) (adverb +) (adjective +) noun + relative clause
ˏJane, | I'd ˙like you to ˙meet a 'very ˙nice ˙young ˏman I ˙know.

1.1.11 NP denoting container (6.4.2) or measure (6.2.8.2, 4, 5, 6.4.2) + of + NP denoting mass substances, materials or plurals
I'd ˙like a 'pound of ˏapples | and a 'large ˙bottle of ˙dry ˙white ˏwine.

1.2 **Use of noun phrases**

1.2.1 as subject (6.7.3.1, 2, 3)
The 'young ˏwoman | 'ran aˏway.

1.2.2 as direct object of transitive verb (6.7.3.2)
We ˏwon | the ˏfootball ˙match.

1.2.3 as indirect object of verb of giving (6.7.3.3)
I 'gave my ˏsister | a 'CˏD ˙player.

1.2.4 in prepopositional phrases
We ˙went to a 'fine ˙old ˏhouse.

1.3 **Use**
At *Threshold Level*, learners should be able to understand all the types of noun phrase shown above. They may be expected to produce them, however, only in fixed combinations they have met, or else in relatively simple form, with not more than, say, two qualifying elements in addition to the basic determiner + noun.

B 2 **Adjective phrases**

2.1 **Forms (in addition to those in B 1.1.7 and 1.1.8 above)**

2.1.1 predicative adjective + post-modifier
This ˙food is 'not ˏgood e·nough.

2.1.2 predicative adjective + adjunct
'Smoking is ˏbad for you.

2.1.3 predicative complementising adjective + complement phrase or clause (cf. C 2.1.1.1 below)
ᵛApples | are 'good to ˏeat.
It is 'probable that he will ˏcome.

2.2 **Use**
At *Threshold Level*, learners should be able to recognise the types of adjectival phrase shown and to produce them in simple form.

B 3 **Pronoun phrase**

3.1 **Forms**

3.1.1 determiner + adjective + one(s) (6.8.1.2)
'Give me the ˏlargest one(s).

3.1.2 some + of + determiner + mass noun/plural noun
I'd 'like some of the ˌbutter, ·please.

3.1.3 indefinite pronoun (6.8.2) + adjunct
'May I have ·something to ˌdrink?

3.1.4 indefinite pronoun + adjective
He told me 'nothing ·new or ˌinteresting.

3.1.5 indefinite pronoun + relative clause
'Susan is ·someone I ·met in ˌSpain.

3.2 Use
At *Threshold Level*, learners should be able to understand the above types of pronominal phrase and to produce them in simple form.

....

B 4 Verb phrase (VP)

4.1 Forms containing one main verb

4.1.1 intransitive verb (6.2.4)
The ˌtrain ar·rived.

4.1.2 copula + NP complement (5.1.1)
'This ˌanimal | is a ˌdog.

4.1.3 transitive verb + NP direct object (6.7.3.2)
I ·saw a ˌbird.

4.1.4 transitive verb + NP direct object (6.7.3.2) + NP indirect object (6.7.3.3)
I 'showed the ·letter to his ˌmother.
(+ benefactive 6.7.3.5)
I 'gave ·John the ·letter for ˌMarion.

(+ instrumental 6.7.3.4)
·Susan 'opened the ˌdoor for me | with her ˌkey.

4.1.5 adverb + verb
'He and ˌI | 'always aˌgree.

4.1.6 verb + adverb(s)
He 'walked ˌhome a·gain | 'very ˌslowly ·afterwards.

4.1.7 copula + adjectival phrase
She is 'very inˌtelligent.

4.1.8 copula + adverb
The 'fork is ˌhere.

4.1.9 copula + prepositional phrase
The 'cup is on the ˌtable.

4.1.10 stative verb + complement NP
She ·seems a 'nice ˌgirl.

4.1.11 stative verb + adjectival phrase
The ·fish ·tastes 'very ˌnice.

4.1.12 verb + prepositional or adverbial particle (phrasal verb)
The 'dog is ·lying ˌdown.

4.1.13 verb + adverbial (prepositional) adjunct
Our 'guests ·sleep in ˌthis ·bedroom.

4.2 Short answers (5.1.5, 5.2.1) auxiliary or pro-verb only

4.2.1 be
('Are you ˌFrench?) ˌYes, I ˌam.

4.3.2 have
('Has he ˌfinished?) ˌYes, | he ˌhas.

4.2.3 modals
('Can I ˌgo now?) ˌYes, | you ˌcan.

4.2.4 do
('Do they like ˌmutton?) ˌNo, | they ˌdon't.

4.3   Pro-verb phrase do so
He 'asked me to ‚stop | and I ‚did
so.

**4.4   Nominalised verb phrases
(VPs)**

4.4.1   to + VP infinitive
I 'want to ·go ‚home.

4.4.2   wh + to + VP infinitive
I ·don't ·know 'what to ‚do.

4.4.3   VP gerund
I 'like ·swimming in the ‚sea.

**4.5   Use of nominalised verb
phrases**

4.5.1   to + infinitive

4.5.1.1   as subject ⓡ
To ˅kill ·people | is ‚wrong.

**4.5.1.2   following complementising
adjectives (cf. A 4.5 above) of
probability (5.2.9, 10)**
It is 'likely to ‚rain to·morrow.
of certainty (5.2.13, 14)
He is ex'pected to ar·rive ‚late.
of evaluation (6.5.2)
It is 'wrong to ‚kill ·people.
**denoting emotional states
(5.2.29–50)**
I am 'glad to ‚see you.
**denoting physical qualities
(6.5.1)**
This ·bed is ‚soft to ·lie on.
**denoting moral qualities
(5.2.49)**
It is ˋkind of you | to in‚vite us.
denoting order (6.3.9)
They are 'always the ‚last to
ar·rive.
denoting availability (6.1.3)
'Is the ·food ·ready to ‚eat?

**4.5.1.3   with adjectives and adverbs of
degree (6.4.3)**
enough
The 'tea is ·now ·cool e·nough to
‚drink. 'Have you had e·nough to
‚eat?

too
My ·grandfather is 'too ‚old | to
‚travel.
very
This ·case is 'very ‚heavy to ·carry.

**4.5.1.4   following certain
complementising
verbs (cf. A 7.1.7 above)
forget, remember**
'Did you re·member to ·close the
‚window?
verbs of volition (5.2.23–27)
I 'want to be·come a ‚doctor.
**verbs expressing emotions
(5.2.29–46)**
I 'hope to ‚pass the exami·nation.
commencement (6.3.24)
It is be'ginning to ‚rain.
suasion (6.6.2)
'Tell him to ·come ‚here.
appearance (5.2.13)
She 'seems to be a‚sleep.

**4.5.1.5   following an indefinite
pronoun (6.8.2)**
I 'want ·something to ‚eat.

**4.5.1.6   following an indefinite
adverb (6.8.2)**
I have 'nowhere to ‚sleep.

4.5.2   wh + to + VP infinitive

**4.5.2.1   following certain
complementising adjectives
certain (5.2.13)**
'Are you ·certain ·where to ‚go?

**4.5.2.2   following certain
complementising verbs
denoting cognitive attitudes
(5.2) tell, teach**
'Do you ·know ·where to ‚go?
'Teach me ·how to ‚swim.

4.5.3   VP gerund

4.5.3.1   as subject
'Swimming in the ‚sea | 'can be
‚dangerous.

4.5.3.2 following certain complementising verbs

forget, remember (5.2.7, 8)
I'll 'never forget ·meeting the ·Prime ‚Minister.

like, intend, prefer (5.2.23–28)
She pre·fers ‚driving | to ·going by ‚train.

love, hate, enjoy (5.2.32–34)
I 'quite en‚joy | ·travelling by ‚air.

stop, finish (6.3.25)
At 'last it has ·stopped ‚raining.

4.5.3.3 in prepositional phrases ®
I 'don't be‚lieve | in ·punishing ·little ‚children.
'Don't ‚leave | without 'paying the ‚bill.

4.6 Use

Learners at *Threshold Level* should be able to understand the verb phrases listed above and to use them productively as exponents of the functional and notional categories set out in Chapters 5, 6 and 7. It will be seen that since the verb phrase comprises everything in the sentence apart from the subject NP it is capable of very great complexity. The ability of learners at *Threshold Level* to process complex syntactic structures receptively is limited and their ability to produce them very much more so. Whilst it is not possible to list *in extenso* the combinations a learner at *Threshold Level* will be able to understand or produce beyond the relatively fixed collocations which are the direct exponents of particular functions, it is recommended that meaningful content should be spread over a number of relatively simple sentences, or, in the case of conversation, a number of relatively simple contributions from the partners in turn, rather than organised into longer and more complex sentences.

B 5 Adverbial phrase

5.1 adverb of degree and gradable adverb
He ·drove 'very ‚fast.

5.2 comparative of equality/inequality
He ·did as 'well as he ‚could.

5.3 prepositional phrase(s)
We 'drove to the ‚seaside | by ‚car.

B 6 Preposition phrase

(*Note* We mean by this a phrase fulfilling the function of a preposition, not an adverbial consisting of a preposition + a noun phrase, often termed a prepositional phrase.)

6.1 Preposition + NP + of

6.1.1 in front of (6.2.2)
The 'bus ·stop is in ·front of the ‚bank.

6.1.2 in the centre of (6.2.2)
The ca'thedral is in the ·centre of the ‚city.

6.1.3 at the back of (7.4.4)
The 'plates are at the ·back of the ‚cupboard.

6.1.4 **at/to the side of (6.2.2)**
'Put the ˌknife | to the 'side of the
ˌplate.

6.1.5 **at the end of (6.2.2)**
Their ·house is at the 'end of the
ˌroad.

6.1.6 **to the left/right of (6.2.5)**
The 'fridge is to the ·right of the
ˌwashing-ma·chine.

6.1.7 **in the neighbourhood of (6.2.3)**
'Sonning is in the
·neighbourhood of ˌReading.

6.2 **Adverb and preposition**

6.2.1 **next to (6.2.2)**
We 'live ·next to an ˌactor.

6.2.2 **far (away) from (6.2.3)**
The ·house is 'not ·far from the
ˌshops.

6.2.3 **out of (6.2.6)**
An 'animal came ·out of the
ˌforest.

C   Clause level

C 1   Clause types and functions

1.1 **Main clause (NP and finite VP)**

1.1.1 **as sole constituent of a simple sentence** (See D 1.1 below.)
I will 'come ·home ˌsoon.

1.1.2 **as co-ordinate constituent of a compound sentence**
My work is 'nearly ˌfinished | and I will 'come ˌhome | ˌsoon.

1.1.3 **as main clause in a complex sentence**
I will 'come ˌhome | when my ˌwork is ·finished.

1.2 **Subordinate clause**

1.2.1 **as short answer to a *wh-* question**
('When are you ·coming ˌhome?)
'When my ˌwork is ·finished.

1.2.2 **as part of a complex sentence**
I 'left when my ˌwork was ·finished.

C 2   Forms and functions of subordinate clauses

2.1   **Noun clauses**

2.1.1 **(that) + NP + VP finite**

2.1.1.1 **following it + be + adjective of probability (5.2.9, 10)**
It is 'likely that it will ˌsnow | to,night.
certainty (5.2.13, 14)
It is ex'pected that the ·teachers will ˌstrike.
evaluation (6.5.2)
It is 'good that he has ˌcome.

2.1.1.2 **following it + certain complementising verbs matter (5.2.39)**
It 'doesn't ˌmatter | that she is ·not ˌhere.
surprise (5.2.41)
It sur'prises me | that he has ˌleft al·ready.

2.1.1.3 **following it + be + certain noun phrases**
It is a ˋpity | (that) they cannot ˌcome.

2.1.1.4 **following certain complementising adjectives (cf. A 4.5 above)**
certainty (5.2.13, 14)
I am 'sure (that) he will ˌcome.
denoting emotional states (5.2.29–50)
I am ˌsorry | (that) she is ˌill.
expressing surprise (5.2.41)
I am sur'prised | (that) he 'loves ˋher.

2.1.1.5 following certain complementising verbs cf. A 7.1.7 above)
reporting (5.1.2)
He ·said that the ·food was 'very ‚good.
knowing (5.2.5, 6)
I 'know (that) she ·works in an ‚office.
remembering (5.2.7, 8)
I re'member (that) he is ·very ‚tall.
expressing certainty (5.2.13, 14)
Do you 'think (that) it will be ‚foggy?
expressing hope (5.2.44)
I ‘do ·hope | (that) you will ·come to ‚dinner.

2.1.2 if + NP + VP finite

2.1.2.1 in indirect questions, following verbs of:
asking
She 'asked if he was ‚ready yet.
wondering
I 'wonder if you could ‚help me.
knowing
I 'don't ·know if you will ‚like ·this.

2.1.3 *wh* clause (*wh* + NP + VP)

2.1.3.1 as subject
'What I ‚like | is 'watching ‚football.

2.1.3.2 as complement after *be*
This is 'not what I ex‚pected | or ‚wanted.

2.1.3.3 in indirect questions, following verbs of:
asking
I 'asked him ·where he was ‚going.
wondering
I 'wonder where my ‚keys are.
telling
I 'told him when the ·train was ‚leaving.

remembering
I have for‘gotten | ·when he was ‚born.
knowing
I 'don't ·know ‘why | he ‚left her.

2.1.4 what + VP

2.1.4.1 as subject
'What ‚interests me | is ‚politics.

2.1.4.2 as object
I ‚know | what is ‚meant.

2.1.5 NP + VP infinitive

2.1.5.1 following verbs of sensory perception
I 'saw him ·drive a‚way.

2.1.5.2 following causative have ®
I 'had the ‚laundry ·clean my ·raincoat.

2.1.6 NP + to + VP infinitive

2.1.6.1 following verbs of volition (5.2.23–27)
I 'want my ·son to be·come a ‚doctor.
liking (5.2.32–34)
I 'do not ·like my ·children to ‚smoke.
suasion (6.6.2)
'Tell that ·man not to ‚smoke in ·here.
cognition (5.2.5–8) ®
I 'know him to be a ‚kind ·man.

2.1.7 NP + VP gerund

2.1.7.1 following verbs of remembering (5.2.7, 8)
I re'member my ‚brother being ·born.
liking and disliking (5.2.23–28)
I 'hate ·insects ·eating my ‚vegetables.

2.1.8 NP (+ to be) + adjective ®
I pre'fer ·water (to be) ‚boiled.

2.1.9 pro-clause so

2.1.9.1 following certain complementising verbs
of reflection (6.6.1)
('Will he ˎcome?) I ˅hope/˅think/
be˅lieve so.
of expression (6.6.2)
('Is she ˎreally ·French?) She ˅says
so.

2.2 Adjectival (relative) clauses

2.2.1 following NP human

2.2.1.1 who + VP
'This is the ·man who ˎlives with
me.

2.2.1.2 that + VP
'This is the ·woman that
de·feated me at ˎchess.

2.2.1.3 whom + NP + VP ®
'Alison is the ·girl whom I ·met in
ˎTurkey.

2.2.1.4 (that) + NP + VP
'She is the ·actress (that) I ·like
ˎbest.

**2.2.1.5 preposition + whom + NP
+ VP ®**
'Mrs. ˎSmith I is a ·lady with
whom I ˎwork.

**2.2.1.6 (who/that) + NP + VP
preposition**
'Joe's a ·man (who/that) I ·play
ˎrugby with.

2.2.1.7 (possessive) whose + NP + VP ®
The 'man whose ·daughter
·taught me ˎFrench has ·just
·died.

2.2.1.8 whose + NP + NP + VP ®
'This is a ·colleague whose ·wife I
·trained as a ˎnurse.

2.2.2 following NP non-human

2.2.2.1 which/that + VP
I 'read a ·book which/that
ex·plains ·nuclear ˎphysics.

2.2.2.2 which/that + NP + VP
'Have you seen the ˎcar
which/that I ·bought?

2.2.3 following superlative

2.2.3.1 (that) NP + VP
Is 'that the ·best (that) you can
ˎdo?

**2.2.4 restrictive and non-restrictive
relative clauses**

2.2.4.1 restrictive
I 'do not buy ·books which are
ˎboring. (i.e. I only buy
interesting books.)

2.2.4.2 non-restrictive
I 'do not ˎbuy ˎbooks, | which are
ˎboring. (i.e. I do not buy any
books, because all books are
boring.)

2.3 Adverbial clauses

2.3.1 of place (6.2)

2.3.1.1 where ... (6.2.2)
It 'hurts where I ·put my ˎfinger.

2.3.2 of time (6.3), denoting

**2.3.2.1 point of time (6.3.3, 6.3.10)
when**
'Please ˎcome when I ·call you.

2.3.2.2 duration (past) (6.3.4) since
It is ˎquiet ·here | since ˎIan ·left.

**2.3.2.3 duration (future) (6.3.4,
6.3.25) until ®/till**
I will ('not) ˎsleep | un'til/till he
reˎturns.

2.3.2.4 anteriority (6.3.8) before
The 'accident ·happened be·fore
I arˎrived.

2.3.2.5 posteriority (6.3.8) after
'After we ·finished ˎeating, | we
'paid the ˎbill.

**2.3.2.6 simultaneity (at point in time)
(6.3.10) as soon as**
'Tell me as ·soon as the ·boat
ˎsails.

2.3.2.7 simultaneity (duration)
(6.3.10) **while**
There will be a 'short de‚lay |
while we 'check the ‚plane.

2.3.3 expressing logical relations
(6.7)

2.3.3.1 reason, cause (6.7.6.4) **because**
I ·eat ‚brown ·bread | be·cause it
is ‚good for me.

2.3.3.2 cause (6.7.6.4) **as ®**
'As he was ‚tired, | he 'lost the
‚match.

2.3.3.3 reason (6.7.6.6) **since ®**
'Since you are ‚sorry, | I'll
for‚give you.

2.3.3.4 effect (6.7.6.5) **so**
He 'turned ‚right, | so he 'lost his
‚way.

2.3.3.5 effect (6.7.6.5) **so ... (that)**
The ·suitcase was 'so ‚heavy |
(that) I 'couldn't ‚carry it.

2.3.3.6 condition (6.7.6.8) **if**
(See also 5.2.20, 39, 57.)
'If you ‚like, | ‚you can ·come |
‚too.

2.3.3.7 comparison (6.7.4.2) **than**
The ·tea is 'stronger than I had
ex‚pected.
as ... as ®
He ·works as 'hard as he ‚can.
not so ... as ®
He is 'not so in‚telligent | as he
‚thinks he ·is.

D Sentence level

D 1 Form

1.1 **Simple sentences, consisting
of one main clause (cf. C 1.1.1
above)**

1.2 **Compound sentences,
consisting of two or more
main clauses, linked by
co-ordinating conjunctions
(cf. A 8.1 above)**

1.3 **Complex sentences,
consisting of a main clause +
one or more subordinate
clauses (cf. C 1.2 above)**

D 2 Sentence types

2.1 **Declarative**

2.1.1 affirmative
The 'tourists ·ate their
‚sandwiches.

2.1.1.1 emphatic affirmative (5.1.3)
NP + *do* + VP infinitive
I `did ·tell you.

2.1.2 negative

2.1.2.1 NP + *be/have* + not/n't + ...
It 'isn't ·cold in ˇAfrica.

2.1.2.2 NP + *do*/modal + n't + VP
infinitive
It 'doesn't ·rain in the Sa·hara
ˇdesert.
He 'can't speak ˇFrench.

2.1.2.3 with negative indefinite
pronouns, adverbs, etc. (6.8.2)
'Nobody ‚likes me.
'Old ‚soldiers | 'never ‚die.

2.1.2.4 use of negative expression + indefinite pronoun, adverb, etc.
He 'won't ·eat ˌanything.
'Nobody is ·safe ˌanywhere.

2.2 Interrogative

2.2.1 decision (yes/no) questions

2.2.1.1 be/have (+ not) + NP + ...
'Are you ˌready?
'Haven't you ·been to ˌItaly?

2.2.1.2 do/modal (+ not) + NP + infinitive
'Don't you ·eat ˌmeat?
'Can I ˌhelp you?

2.2.1.3 declarative sentence with high-rising intonation
You're ′ready?

2.2.1.4 affirmative sentence + negative tag question with falling intonation conducive to the answer 'yes'
You 'are ˌcoming, | ˌaren't you?
with low-rising intonation non-conducive
You are ˌGerman, | ˌaren't you?

2.2.1.5 negative sentence + positive tag with falling intonation conducive to the answer 'no'
You 'don't aˌgree with her, | ˌdo you?
with low-rising intonation, non-conducive
Jane 'hasn't ˌleft yet, | ˌhas she?

2.2.2 special questions (wh) requiring an answer consisting in or containing:

2.2.2.1 a subject NP (human)
Who + VP finite
'Who has ·drunk my ˌtea?
(ˇSorry, ˋI ·have.)

2.2.2.2 a subject NP (non-human)
What + VP finite
'What ·interests you ˌmost?
(ˌPolitics.)

2.2.2.3 specification of a subject NP
Which + NP + VP finite
'Which ·driver ·owns this ˌcar?
(ˌMe.)

2.2.2.4 an object NP (human)
Who/Whom ❽ + auxiliary + NP + VP non-finite, containing a transitive verb
'Who did you ˌsee ·last ·night?
'Whom did you ˌsee ·last ·night?

2.2.2.5 an object NP (non-human)
What + auxiliary + NP + VP non-finite containing a transitive verb
'What do you ·want for ˌbreakfast?

2.2.2.6 a specified object NP
Which + NP + auxiliary + NP + VP non-finite, containing a transitive verb
'Which ·food do you ·like ˌbest?

2.2.2.7 an adverbial of time
When + interrogative sentence structure
'When does the ·train ˌleave?

2.2.2.8 an adverbial of place
Where + interrogative sentence structure
'Where did you ·go ˌafterwards?

2.2.2.9 an adverbial of manner
How + interrogative sentence structure
'How can I ·pay the ˌbill?

2.2.2.10 an adverbial of reason (or relative declarative sentence)
Why + auxiliary + interrogative sentence
'Why do you ·go to ˌchurch?
(Be·cause I be'lieve in ˌGod.)
Why are you a·fraid of the 'poˌlice?
(I 'don't 'know, | but ...)

2.3 Imperative

2.3.1 VP infinitive
'Go to ·bed at ˌonce.

2.3.2 you + VP infinitive ®
ˌJohn, | ·you be a 'good ˌboy |
and 'eat your ˌspinach!

2.3.3 do + VP infinitive
'Do ·please ·sit ˌdown!

2.3.4 let's + VP infinitive
'Let's ·go to the ˌtheatre!

....

D 3 Functions of sentence types

3.1 Affirmative sentences

3.1.1 reporting (5.1.2)

3.1.1.1 narrating an event (5.1.2)
The ·flight ar·rived at '9 a.ˌm.

3.1.1.2 describing (5.1.2)
ᵛSue | has 'blue ˌeyes.

3.1.2 answering questions (5.1.5)
It ·happened 'early this ˌmorning.

3.1.3 making statements concerning:

3.1.3.1 agreement (5.2.1)
I 'quite aˌgree with you.

3.1.3.2 knowledge (5.2.5)
I 'know he was ·here ˌyesterday.

3.1.3.3 memory (5.2.7)
I re'member ˌmeeting you | in
'198ˌ5.

3.1.3.4 probability (5.2.9)
I am 'likely to ·see him in
ˌLondon.

3.1.3.5 logical necessity (5.2.11)
'Casa ᵛVecchia | 'must be in
ˋItaly.

3.1.3.6 certainty (5.2.13)
I am 'sure he will ˌcome.

3.1.3.7 obligation (5.2.15)
You 'must ·stay here ·till I
reˌturn.

3.1.3.8 ability (5.2.17)
'All ·young ˌSwedes | can 'speak
ˌEnglish.

3.1.3.9 permissibility (5.2.19)
'Parking is alˌlowed | from
'6 ·p.ˌm. | to '8 ·a.ˌm.

3.1.4 expressing:

3.1.4.1 wants and desires (5.2.23)
I 'want to ·see my ˌfriend.

3.1.4.2 intentions (5.2.25)
I am 'going to ·buy a ·new ˌcar.

3.1.4.3 preference (5.2.27)
I'd 'rather ˋdie | than ·give ·up
ˌtennis.

3.1.4.4 pleasure, happiness (5.2.29)
I'm de'lighted to ˌsee you a·gain.

3.1.4.5 displeasure, unhappiness (5.2.30)
I'm ·feeling 'very ˌmiserable this
·morning.

3.1.4.6 liking (5.2.32)
I 'like ·cakes and ˌpastries | 'very
ˌmuch.

3.1.4.7 dislike (5.2.33)
'This ᵛcoffee | ·tastes ˋhorrible.

3.1.4.8 satisfaction (5.2.35)
This ·brandy is 'just what I ˌneed.

3.1.4.9 dissatisfaction (5.2.36)
The 'shower in the ˌbathroom | is
'not ˌworking.

3.1.4.10 interest (5.2.38)
I am 'very ·interested in ·old
ˌbuildings.

3.1.4.11 lack of interest (5.2.39)
I ·don't ·care if it ·rains 'all ˌday.

3.1.4.12 surprise (5.2.41)
I'm surˋprised | he ·didn't
ˌphone.

3.1.4.13 hope (5.2.44)
I 'hope to be·come an ˌactress.

3.1.4.14 fear (5.2.46)
I'm aˌfraid | of the ˌdark.

3.1.4.15 gratitude (5.2.49)
I'm 'very ·grateful to you for ˌhelping me.

3.1.4.16 moral obligation (5.2.53)
You should be 'kind to ˌanimals.

3.1.4.17 regret (5.2.57)
I'm 'very ˌsorry | that I ·broke your ˌwindow.

3.1.4.18 sympathy (5.2.57)
I'm ˋso ·sorry | to ·hear your ˌwife is ·ill.

3.1.5   giving:

3.1.5.1 suggestions (5.3.1)
We 'might per·haps ·go to ˌTurkey ·this ·year.

3.1.5.2 advice (5.3.4)
You 'ought to ·see a ˌdoctor.

3.1.5.3 warning (5.3.5)
This ·plate is 'very ˌhot.

3.1.5.4 instructions (5.3.7)
You 'cut the ·paper ·like ˌthis.

3.1.5.5 directions (5.3.7)
The ·party will ·meet 'outside the hoˌtel | at '5.·30 ·a.ˌm.

3.1.6   structuring discourse by

3.1.6.1 introducing a theme (5.5.4)
I'd 'like to ·say ·something about ·world ˌpoverty.

3.1.6.2 expressing an opinion (5.5.5)
In 'my oˌpinion, | 'nuclear ·weapons are ˌuseless.

3.1.6.3 giving emphasis (5.5.8)
I 'must ·stress the ˌfact | that we are ˌfriends.

3.1.6.4 repeating what one has said (5.6.13)
I ·said that I ·wanted a ˋdrink, ·please.

3.2   Emphatic affirmative sentences

3.2.1   correcting a negative statement (5.1.3)
But I ˋdid ·see him!

3.2.2   expressing certainty (5.2.13)
I'm 'sure he ˌdoes ·eat ·cheese.

3.2.3   expressing strong positive feelings
I 'do like ·ice-ˇcream!

3.3   Negative sentences

3.3.1   correcting a positive statement (5.1.3)
'No, I ˇdidn't ·see her.

3.3.2   denying statements (5.2.4)
But I know 'nothing aˌbout it.

3.3.3   denying knowledge, belief, etc. (5.2.5, 13, etc.)
I 'don't ˇthink so.

3.3.4   expressing negative feelings and attitudes (5.2.30, 33, 36, etc.)
I 'don't like ·hot ˌmilk.

3.3.5   withholding permission (5.2.19, 22)
You 'cannot go ˌout to·night.

3.4   Decision questions

3.4.1   asking for confirmation (5.1.4)
You ˋwon, | ˋdidn't you?

3.4.2   enquiring about:

3.4.2.1 agreement (5.2.3)
'Don't you ·think that's ˌdangerous?

3.4.2.2 knowledge (5.2.6)
'Do you ·know my ˌcousin?

3.4.2.3 memory (5.2.8)
'Do you re·member the ˌwar?

3.4.2.4 probability (5.2.10)
'Are you ·likely to ·vote ˌLabour?

3.4.2.5 necessity (5.2.12)
'Must you ·leave alˌready?

3.4.2.6 certainty (5.2.14)
'Are you ·sure it has ·stopped ˌraining? 'Do you ·really ˌthink so?

3.4.2.7 ability (5.2.18)
'Are you ·able to ˌsee?

3.4.2.8 permissibility (5.2.20)
'Is it all ·right if I ·open the ˌwindow?

3.4.3 enquiring about:

3.4.3.1 wants, desires (5.2.24)
'Would you ·like to ˌdance?

3.4.3.2 intentions (5.2.26)
'Are you ·thinking of ·getting ˌup?

3.4.3.3 preferences (5.2.28)
'Do you pre·fer ·orange-·juice to ˌbeer?

3.4.3.4 feelings (5.2.31, 34, 37, 40, 43, 48, 56)
'Do you ·like my ·new ˌhat?

3.4.4 making requests (5.3.3)
'Could you ·open the ˌwindow, ·please?

3.4.5 asking for help (5.3.8)
'Can you ˌhelp me, ·please?

3.4.6 offering assistance (5.3.9)
'Can I ˌhelp you?

3.5 Special (*wh*) questions

3.5.1 asking for specific information (5.1.3)
'How ·far is it to the ˌstation?

3.5.2. asking about wants and desires (5.2.24)
'Where would you ·like to ˌgo?

3.5.3 asking for preferences (5.2.8)
'Which do you preˌfer, | 'coffee or ˌtea?

3.5.4 enquiring about well-being (5.2.31)
'How are you ˌfeeling?

3.5.5 enquiring about satisfaction (5.2.37) approval (5.2.56)
'How do you ·find our ˌfood?

3.5.6 giving advice (5.3.4)
'Why don't you ·go to ˌbed?

3.6 Imperative sentences

3.6.1 asking for information (5.1.4)
'Tell me what ˌhappened.

3.6.2 giving reassurance (5.2.47)
'Don't be aˌfraid.

3.6.3 apologising (5.2.51)
'Please forˌgive me | for ˌhurting you.

3.6.4 making suggestions (5.3.1)
'Let's go ·out for a ˌmeal.

3.6.5 making requests (5.3.3)
'Please ·make ·less ˌnoise!

3.6.6 giving warnings (5.3.5)
'Don't for·get your ˇpassport!

3.6.7 offering assistance (5.3.9)
'Let me ˌhelp you.

3.6.8 giving encouragement (5.3.6)
'Go ˌon, 'ring him ˌup!

3.6.9 giving instructions or directions (5.3.7)
'Put a ·little ·salt and ˌpepper on the ·omelette.

D 4   Use

At *Threshold Level,* learners should be able to understand and produce simple sentences within the limits of the *Threshold Level* specification, given that noun and verb phrases are not overloaded (cf. D 1.3 and B 4.6 above). Within the same limits they should be able to understand and produce compound sentences. They can be expected to produce complex sentences which are straightforward in character, e.g. limited to one subordinate clause of fairly simple structure with a main clause frame of a basic character, as for instance in the examples in this summary. Learners should be able to understand complex sentences containing more than one embedded clause, given that the internal structure of clauses and the relations between them are uncomplicated. It is difficult to define exact limits. Any learner who has attained *Threshold Level* competence should have little difficulty with such sentences as

> He ·said he 'wanted to ˌleave.
> 'When I ˌleft, | I 'saw that it was ˌraining.

> or even:
> We 'thought you were ˌill | be·cause you ·said you had a ˌheadache.

An experienced and literate reader will perhaps be able to handle textual material of greater complexity and most learners will be able to achieve gist and single point comprehension in dealing with such texts. Listening comprehension is more demanding and the chain of understanding may be broken if the speech presented under conditions where repair strategies cannot be used is too complicated or too dense. In writing, simplicity is generally a virtue. In conversation, learners should be able to understand the interlocutor's contributions where they are short and within the limits of this specification. Where that is not the case, they should be able to operate repair strategies, using the expressions given in 5.6 (see also Chapter 12). Their own contributions may be expected to be relatively short, with short answers consisting of single phrases and clauses, simple sentences or the simplest of complex sentences. These simple means should, however, be sufficient to ensure communication at a basic level.

Appendix C Word index

boat *n*: **7.5.1**
boil *vb*: **6.2.8.7, 7.10.1**
bomb *n*: **7.6.6, 7.6.7**
book *n*: **7.4.6**
book *vb*: **7.5.1, 7.5.5**
booking office *n*: **7.4.4, 7.5.1**
bookshop *n*: **7.4.6**
booth *n*: **7.11.2**
border *n*: **7.5.7**
bored *adj*: **5.2.39.2**
boring *adj*: **5.2.39.1**
born *adj*: **7.1.4**
borrow *vb*: **7.11.4**
boss *n*: **7.1.10**
both *pr adj*: **6.4.2, 6.8.2**
bottle *n*: **6.4.2, 7.9.5**
bottom *n*: **7.2.7**
box *n*: **6.4.2, 7.5.6, 7.11.1**
boy *n*: **7.1.6**
boy-friend *n*: **7.6.1**
brake *n*: **7.11.8**
bread *n*: **7.10.1**
break *n*: **7.3.2**
break *vb*: **6.5.1.11, 7.7.4**
breakfast *n*: **7.3.1, 7.5.5, 7.10.1**
bridge *n*: **7.5.3**
(in) brief *adj*: **5.5.9.2**
bright *adj*: **6.5.1.9**
bring *vb*: **6.2.5**
brother *n*: **7.1.11**
brown *adj*: **6.5.1.9**
brush *n*: **7.7.3**
Brussels *n*: **7.1.2**
building *n*: **7.2.1**
bullet *n*: **7.6.7**
bureau *n*: **7.5.1**
burglar *n*: **7.6.6**
burglary *n*: **7.6.6**
burn *vb*: **6.2.8.7, 7.7.4**
bus *n*: **7.5.1**
bush *n*: **7.2.8**
business *n*: **7.5.1**
business-man *n*: **7.1.10**
business-woman *n*: **7.1.10**
but *conj*: **5.2.22.4, 6.7.6.1**
butcher *n*: **7.1.10, 7.9.1**
butter *n*: **7.10.1**

button *n*: **7.5.5**
buy *vb*: **7.1.10, 7.2.1**
by *prep*: **7.5.1**
by all means *adv*: **5.5.16.2**
bye-bye *int*: **5.4.12.2.1**

C [siː]

cab *n*: **7.5.1**
cabaret *n*: **7.4.4**
cabbage *n*: **7.10.1**
cabin *n*: **7.5.1**
cable *n*: **7.4.3**
café *n*: **7.10.2**
cake *n*: **7.10.1**
call *vb*: **5.5.2.2, 5.5.26, 5.6.9.2, 6.6.10.4,
     7.1.1, 7.1.3, 7.5.5**
call-box *n*: **7.11.2**
camera *n*: **7.5.6**
camp *n*: **7.5.5**
camp site *n*: **7.5.5**
can *vb*: **5.2.9.8, 5.2.10.3, 5.2.17.1, 5.2.19.3,
     5.2.20.1, 5.2.23.6, 5.3.3.7, 5.3.8.1, 5.3.9.2,
     5.3.14.2, 6.5.2.10**
canal *n*: **7.2.7**
cancel *vb*: **7.5.1**
cannot (can't) *vb*: **5.2.7.1, 5.2.9.8,
     5.2.11.2, 5.2.22.2, 5.3.12.2, 6.5.2.10**
canteen *n*: **7.3.2, 7.10.2**
car *n*: **7.5.2**
card *n*: **7.4.7, 7.5.5, 7.9.6**
care *vb*: **5.2.39.6**
careful *adj*: **5.3.5.1**
carpentry *n*: **7.4.2**
carrot *n*: **7.10.1**
carry *vb*: **6.2.5**
cash *n and vb*: **7.5.5, 7.11.4**
cassette *n*: **7.4.3**
cassette recorder *n*: **7.4.3**
castle *n*: **7.5.4**
cat *n*: **7.2.8**
cathedral *n*: **7.1.12, 7.5.4**
cauliflower *n*: **7.10.1**
CD [siːdiː] *n*: **7.4.3**
cellar *n*: **7.2.2**
centimetre *n*: **6.2.8.2**
central *adj*: **7.2.5**

drink *n* and *vb*: **7.10.1**
drive *vb*: **7.5.2, 7.5.7**
driver *n*: **7.5.1, 7.5.2**
driving licence *n*: **7.5.8**
drugs *n*: **7.6.6**
dry *adj* and *vb*: **6.5.1.3**
dull *adj*: **6.5.1.9**
during *prep*: **6.3.4**
dust *vb*: **6.5.1.13**
Dutch *adj*: **7.13.1**
duty *n*: **7.5.7**
duty-free *adj*: **7.5.7**

E [iː]

each *adj*: **6.4.2, 6.8.2**
early *adj*: **6.3.5**
earn *vb*: **7.3.3**
east *n*: **6.2.1, 6.2.5**
easy *adj*: **6.5.2.13**
eat *vb*: **7.10.1**
economics *n*: **7.8.2**
education *n*: **7.8.1**
egg *n*: **7.10.1**
either *conj*: **6.7.6.1**
elect *vb*: **7.6.5**
election *n*: **7.6.5**
electricity *n*: **7.2.5**
else *adv*: **5.5.10.1, 5.5.11.1, 6.7.4.1**
embassy *n*: **7.11.6**
emergency *n*: **7.4.4**
employee *n*: **7.1.10**
employer *n*: **7.1.10**
empty *adj*: **6.5.1.16, 7.11.9**
end *vb* and *n*: **6.2.2, 6.3.9, 6.3.25**
enemy *n*: **7.6.7**
engine *n*: **7.11.8**
English *n* and *adj*: **5.6.9.3, 5.6.10.1,
  5.6.10.2, 7.13.1**
enjoy *vb*: **5.2.32.2, 5.2.33.4, 5.2.34.1**
enough *adj* and *adv*: **5.2.35.5.4, 5.2.36.8,
  6.4.2, 6.4.3, 6.5.2.5**
enquiry *n*: **7.5.1**
entrance *n*: **7.4.4, 7.8.3**
envelope *n*: **7.6.3**
er ... *int*: **5.5.2.1.1, 5.6.10.6**
especially *adv*: **5.5.8.4.1**

EU *n*: **7.6.5**
Europe *n*: **7.5.4**
European Union *n*: **7.6.5**
even *adv*: **6.4.3**
evening *n*: **5.4.2.2, 6.3.2**
ever *adv*: **5.2.4.3, 6.3.17**
every *adj*: **6.3.17**
everybody *pron*: **6.8.2**
everything *pron*: **6.8.2**
everywhere *adv*: **6.2.1, 6.8.2**
exactly *adv*: **5.2.1.5, 5.5.3.4**
examination *n*: **7.8.3**
example *n*: **5.5.7.1**
excellent *adj*: **5.2.54.2, 6.5.2.2**
except *prep*: **6.7.6.3**
excuse *vb*: **5.2.51.7, 5.4.1.1, 5.5.14.1**
exhibition *n*: **7.4.5**
exist *vb*: **6.1.1**
exit *n*: **7.4.4, 7.5.3**
expect *vb*: **5.2.42.3, 5.2.43.2, 7.6.2**
expensive *adj*: **6.5.2.1**
explain *vb*: **5.6.6.4, 7.13.1**

F [ef]

fact *n*: **5.5.8.4.5**
factory *n*: **7.1.10, 7.2.7**
fail *vb*: **6.5.2.8, 7.8.3**
failure *n*: **6.5.2.8**
fair *adj*: **7.1.15**
faithfully *adv*: **5.5.28.2**
fall *vb*: **6.2.4, 7.7.4**
false *adj*: **6.5.2.7**
family *n*: **7.1.1, 7.1.11**
fancy (that)! *int*: **5.2.41.3, 5.2.41.7**
far *adv*: **5.1.4.2.1, 6.2.3**
fare *n*: **7.5.1**
farm *n*: **7.1.10, 7.2.7**
farm worker *n*: **7.1.10**
farmland *n*: **7.2.7**
fast *adv*: **5.6.11.2, 6.3.16, 6.7.3.9, 7.5.1**
fasten *vb*: **6.5.1.11**
fat *adj*: **7.1.15**
father *n*: **7.1.11**
fax *n* and *vb*: **7.11.3**
feel *vb*: **5.2.29.3, 5.2.30.3, 5.2.31.2, 7.7.2,
  7.7.4**

know *vb*: **5.2.5, 5.2.6, 5.2.13.1.6, 5.2.13.3.1, 5.5.2.1.2, 6.6.1**

L [el]

labourer *n*: **7.1.10**
lady *n*: **5.5.1.1.1, 7.1.6**
lake *n*: **7.2.7**
lamb *n*: **7.10.1**
lamp *n*: **7.2.3**
land *n*: **7.2.7**
language *n*: **7.13.1**
large *adj*: **6.2.8.1**
last *adj*: **6.3.3, 6.3.13**
last *adv*: **6.2.7**
late *adj*: **6.3.6**
lately *adv*: **6.3.13**
later *adv*: **5.5.26, 6.3.8, 6.3.9, 6.3.15**
laugh *vb*: **6.6.2**
laundry *n*: **7.7.3**
lavatory *n*: **7.2.2, 7.4.4**
law *n*: **7.6.6**
lawn *n*: **7.4.7**
lawyer *n*: **7.6.6**
lazy *adj*: **7.1.14**
lbs (pounds) *n*: **6.2.8.4**
leader *n*: **7.6.5**
learn *vb*: **7.3.5, 7.4.6, 7.8.1**
leather *n*: **6.5.1.14**
leave *n*: **6.2.4**
lecture *n*: **7.8.1**
left *n*, *adj* and *adv*: **6.2.5, 7.5.3, 7.6.5**
leg *n*: **7.7.1**
leisure *n*: **7.4.1**
lemon *n*: **7.10.1**
lend *vb*: **7.11.4**
lesson *n*: **7.8.1**
let *vb*: **5.3.9.1, 7.2.4**
let's *vb*: **5.3.1.1**
letter *n*: **7.1.1, 7.6.3, 7.11.1**
letter-box *n*: **7.11.1**
level *adj*: **7.5.3**
level crossing *n*: **7.5.3**
liberal *n* and *adj*: **7.6.5**
library *n*: **7.4.6**
licence *n*: **7.5.8**
lie down *vb*: **6.2.4**

lift *n*: **7.2.2, 7.5.5**
light *adj*: **6.2.8.3, 6.2.8.4, 6.5.1.4, 6.5.1.9**
light *n*: **7.5.3, 7.11.8**
lightning *n*: **7.14.1**
like *vb*: **5.2.23, 5.2.24, 5.2.32, 5.2.33, 5.2.34, 5.2.36.3, 5.2.36.4, 5.3.10.1, 5.3.11.7, 5.3.14.1, 5.5.4.1, 5.6.12.2, 6.5.2.4, 6.5.2.6**
like *adj*: **6.7.4.2**
likely *adj*: **5.2.9.4, 5.2.9.6, 5.2.9.7, 5.2.10.1, 5.2.10.2**
limit *n*: **7.5.3**
line *n*: **5.5.23.1**
Lisbon *n*: **7.1.2**
listen *vb*: **6.5.1.5, 7.4.3**
litre *n*: **6.2.8.5**
(a) little *pron*: **6.4.2, 6.4.3, 7.13.1**
live *vb*: **7.1.2, 7.7.4**
living *adj*: **7.1.10**
living room *n*: **7.2.2**
locker *n*: **7.5.6**
long *adj*: **5.1.4.2.1, 6.2.8.2, 6.2.8.3**
look *vb*: **5.3.5.1, 6.5.1.4, 6.5.1.11, 7.7.2**
lorry *n*: **7.5.2**
lose *vb*: **7.4.7, 7.5.3, 7.11.5**
lost property office *n*: **7.5.1**
lot *n*: **6.4.2**
a lot *pron*: **6.4.3**
loud *adj*: **6.5.1.5**
lounge *n*: **7.5.1, 7.5.5**
love *n* and *vb*: **5.2.32.3, 5.3.11.7, 5.4.7.2, 5.5.28.1.3**
lovely *adj*: **5.2.29.1**
lover *n*: **7.6.1**
low *adj*: **6.2.8.1, 6.2.8.3, 6.5.2.1**
luggage *n*: **7.5.1, 7.5.6**
lunch *n*: **7.3.1, 7.10.1**
lung *n*: **7.7.1**

M [em]

Madam *n*: **5.4.7.1, 5.5.27.2.1**
magazine *n*: **7.4.8**
mail *n*: **7.11.1**
main *adj*: **7.5.3, 7.10.1**
make *vb*: **6.1.1, 6.5.1.14, 7.3.1, 7.4.6**
male *n* and *adj*: **7.1.6**

N [en]

postcard *n*: **7.6.3**
poste-restante *adv*: **7.11.1**
postman *n*: **7.11.1**
pot *n*: **7.3.1, 7.9.5**
potato *n*: **7.10.1**
poultry *n*: **7.10.1**
pound (lb) *n*: **6.2.8.4**
pound (£) *n*: **7.9.6**
poverty *n*: **7.6.8**
prefer *vb*: **5.2.27, 5.5.28**
prescription *n*: **7.7.5**
present *n*: **6.3.12, 7.6.2**
president *n*: **7.6.5**
press *vb*: **7.5.5**
pretty *adj*: **7.1.15**
price *n*: **6.5.2.1, 7.2.4**
primary *adj*: **7.8.1**
prime *adj*: **7.6.5**
prime minister *n*: **7.6.5**
prince *n*: **7.6.5**
princess *n*: **7.6.5**
prison *n*: **7.6.6**
probable *adj*: **5.2.9.7, 5.2.10.2**
probably *adv*: **5.2.9.2**
problem *n*: **7.6.8**
profession *n*: **7.1.10**
professor *n*: **5.4.6.1, 7.8.1**
programme *n*: **7.4.3, 7.4.4**
pronounce *vb*: **7.13.1**
property *n*: **7.5.1**
pub *n*: **7.10.2**
pull *vb*: **6.2.5, 7.5.5**
punish *vb*: **7.6.6**
punishment *n*: **7.6.6**
pupil *n*: **7.8.1**
purpose *n*: **6.7.6.7**
purse *n*: **7.9.3**
push *vb*: **6.2.5, 7.5.5**
put *vb*: **5.5.2.1.6, 6.2.5**
put on *vb*: **7.9.3**
put through *vb*: **5.5.22.1.2**

Q [kjuː]

qualify *vb*: **7.3.5**
quality *n*: **6.5.2.2**
quarter *n*: **6.3.1, 6.3.2**

quay *n*: **7.5.1**
queen *n*: **7.6.5**
question *n*: **6.6.2, 7.6.8, 7.13.1**
quick *adj*: **6.3.4**
quickly *adv*: **6.7.3.9**
quiet *adj*: **5.5.15.2, 6.5.1.5, 7.1.14**
quilt *n*: **7.2.3**
quite *adv*: **5.2.1.1, 5.2.21.5, 6.4.3**
quiz *n*: **7.4.3**

R [ɑː]

race *n* and *vb*: **7.4.7**
racing *n*: **7.4.7**
radio *n*: **7.2.6, 7.4.3**
railway *n*: **7.5.1**
rain *n* and *vb*: **7.14.1**
raincoat *n*: **7.9.3**
rainy *adj*: **7.14.1**
raisin *n*: **7.10.1**
rank *n*: **7.5.1**
rape *n* and *vb*: **7.6.6**
rarely *adv*: **6.3.17**
rather *adv*: **5.2.27, 5.5.3.6, 6.4.3**
razor *n*: **7.7.3**
reach *vb*: **6.5.1.12**
read *vb*: **7.4.6, 7.4.8, 7.13.1**
reading *n*: **7.8.2**
ready *adj*: **6.1.3**
real *adj*: **6.5.1.15**
really *adv*: **5.2.38.1, 5.5.13.4**
reason *n*: **6.7.6.6**
receipt *n*: **7.5.5**
receive *vb*: **7.6.3**
recently *adv*: **6.3.13**
reception *n*: **7.5.5**
recommend *vb*: **6.6.3**
record *n* and *vb*: **7.4.3**
recorder *n*: **7.4.3**
red *adj*: **6.5.1.9**
refreshments *n*: **7.5.1**
register *n* and *vb*: **7.5.5**
registration *n*: **7.5.5**
religion *n*: **7.1.12**
remain *vb*: **6.3.26**
remember *vb*: **5.2.7, 5.2.8, 6.6.1**
rent *n* and *vb*: **7.2.1, 7.2.4, 7.5.2**
repair *vb*: **6.5.1.11, 7.11.8**

west *n*, *adj* and *adv*: **6.2.1, 6.2.5**
wet *adj*: **6.5.1.2**
what *pron*: **5.1.4.3, 5.2.24.1, 5.5.12.1,**
5.5.12.2, 6.8.1.1
when *adv*: **5.1.4.2.1, 5.1.5.2.1, 6.3.3**
where *adv*: **5.1.4.2.1, 5.1.5.2.2, 5.5.12.3,**
6.2.1, 6.2.2
which *adj*: **5.1.4.3, 6.8.1.1, 6.8.1.2**
while *conj*: **6.3.10**
white *adj*: **6.5.1.9**
who *pron*: **5.1.4.3, 6.8.1.1, 6.8.1.2**
whom *pron*: **6.8.1.1, 6.8.1.2**
whose *adj*: **5.1.4.3, 6.8.1.1, 6.8.1.2**
why *adv*: **5.1.4.2.1, 5.1.3.2.5, 5.2.5.1.2,**
5.2.28.1, 5.3.1.6, 5.3.1.7, 5.3.4.3, 6.7.6.4,
6.7.6.6
wide *adj*: **6.2.8.1**
widow *n*: **7.1.7**
widowed *adj*: **7.1.7**
widower *n*: **7.1.7**
wife *n*: **7.1.11**
will *vb*: **5.2.9.8, 5.2.10.3, 5.2.25.2,**
5.3.13.1, 5.5.2.10, 6.3.11
win *vb*: **7.4.7**
wind *n*: **7.14.1**
window *n*: **7.2.2**
wine *n*: **7.10.1**
wing *n*: **7.6.5**
winter *n*: **6.3.2**
wish *n* and *vb*: **5.5.28.1.2**
with *prep*: **6.2.2, 6.7.5.1, 6.7.6.3**
without *prep*: **6.7.5.1, 6.7.6.3**
witness *n* and *vb*: **7.6.6**
woman *n*: **7.1.6**
wonder *vb*: **5.2.13.3.3, 6.6.1**
wonderful *adj*: **5.2.29.1**
wood *n*: **6.5.1.14, 7.2.7**
wool *n*: **6.5.1.14**
word *n*: **7.11.3**
work *n*: **7.3.1, 7.3.2**

work *vb*: **5.2.36.1, 7.1.10, 7.11.8**
worker *n*: **7.1.10**
working hours *n*: **7.3.2**
(un)worried *adj*: **5.2.46.4, 5.2.48.3**
worry *n* and *vb*: **5.2.47.3, 5.2.48**
worse *adj*: **6.5.2.2**
worst *adj*: **6.5.2.2**
would ('d) *vb*: **5.2.24.1, 5.2.24.2, 5.3.3,**
5.3.10.1
wound *n* and *vb*: **7.7.4**
wrap up *vb*: **7.9.1**
write *vb*: **5.6.8.1, 6.6.2, 7.1.1, 7.4.6, 7.6.3,**
7.13.1
writing *n*: **7.8.2**
wrong *adj*: **5.2.2.3, 6.5.2.3, 6.5.2.7**

X [eks]

Y [wai]

yard *n*: **6.2.8.2**
year *n*: **6.3.2, 6.5.1.10**
yellow *adj*: **6.5.1.9**
yes *int*: **5.1.3.4, 5.1.5.1, 5.2.1.6.1, 5.2.1.6.4,**
5.2.2.5.1, 5.2.21.1, 5.3.11.1, 5.5.13.2
yesterday *n* and *adv*: **6.3.3, 6.3.13**
yet *adv*: **6.3.7**
you *pron*: **5.1.1.1, 5.3.7.1, 6.8.2**
you know *int*: **5.6.10.5**
young *adj*: **6.5.1.10**
your *adj*: **6.7.5.1, 6.8.1.1**
yours *pron*: **6.7.5.1, 6.8.1.2**
yourself *pron*: **6.8.1.2**
youth *n*: **7.5.5**

Z [zed, American ziː]

zero *n*: **6.2.8.7**
zone *n*: **7.5.3**
zoo *n*: **7.5.4**

Open lists

N.B. These categories are 'open' in the sense that we do not try to define a vocabulary for all learners in the areas given. The words a learner needs will depend on circumstances, experience and interests. The examples given in the main text are such as to be likely to be of general use, but learners will need to be able to tell others their own nationality, occupation, etc. even if they are not in the list of examples.

Appendix D   Subject index

Index of language functions and notional categories

In the following index numbers refer to chapters and items or sections. The chapters referred to are 5, 6 and 7. All references beginning with 5 are to language functions, those beginning with 6 to general notions and those beginning with 7 are references to themes or sub-themes.